NICHOLAS WRIGHT

Nicholas Wright's plays include *Vincent in Brixton* (Olivier Award for Best New Play, 2003) and the original production of *Mrs Klein*, at the National Theatre, in the West End and in New York; *The Last of the Duchess* adapted from the book by Caroline Blackwood at Hampstead Theatre; *Rattigan's Nijinsky* at Chichester Festival Theatre; *Travelling Light* at the National Theatre; *A Human Being Died That Night* from the book by Pumla Gobodo-Madikizela at Hampstead Theatre; *Treetops* and *One Fine Day* at Riverside Studios; *The Gorky Brigade* at the Royal Court; *The Crimes of Vautrin* for Joint Stock; *The Custom of the Country* and *The Desert Air* for the RSC; *Cressida* for the Almeida; and *The Reporter* at the National. Adaptations include *His Dark Materials*, *Three Sisters* and *John Gabriel Borkman* for the National; *Thérèse Raquin* at Chichester Festival Theatre and the National; and *Naked* and *Lulu* at the Almeida, where *Mrs Klein* was also revived in 2009. He wrote the ballet scenario for Christopher Wheeldon's *Alice's Adventures in Wonderland* for the Royal Ballet, the libretti for Rachel Portman's opera *The Little Prince* (Houston Grand Opera) and for Jonathan Dove's opera for television, *Man on the Moon*, based on the Apollo 11 Moon landing. Other writing for television includes adaptations of *More Tales of the City* and *The No. 1 Ladies' Detective Agency* (BBC/HBO). His writing about the theatre includes *99 Plays*, a personal view of playwriting from Aeschylus to the present day, and *Changing Stages: A View of British Theatre in the Twentieth Century*, co-written with Richard Eyre.

Pat Barker

REGENERATION

adapted for the stage by
Nicholas Wright

NICK HERN BOOKS
London
www.nickhernbooks.co.uk

A Nick Hern Book

This stage adaptation of *Regeneration* first published in Great Britain in 2014 as a paperback original by Nick Hern Books Limited, The Glasshouse, 49a Goldhawk Road, London W12 8QP

Regeneration copyright © 1991 Pat Barker
First published in Great Britain by Viking Press, 1991
Stage adaptation of *Regeneration* copyright © 2014 Somerset West Ltd

Nicholas Wright has asserted his right to be identified as the author of this adaptation

Cover image: Feast Creative

Designed and typeset by Nick Hern Books, London
Printed and bound in Great Britain by Mimeo Ltd, Huntingdon, Cambridgeshire PE29 6XX

A CIP catalogue record for this book is available from the British Library

ISBN 978 1 84842 440 1

This adaptation of *Regeneration* was first performed at Royal & Derngate, Northampton (James Dacre, Artistic Director; Martin Sutherland, Chief Executive), on 2 September 2014 (previews from 29 August), with the following cast:

ROBERT GRAVES	Christopher Brandon
CAPTAIN RIVERS	Stephen Boxer
CAPTAIN ANDERSON/ DR YEALLAND	Simon Coates
SIEGFRIED SASSOON	Tim Delap
MAJOR CAMPBELL	Joshua Higgott
BILLY PRIOR	Jack Monaghan
CALLAN/ MAJOR WILLARD	David Morley Hale
WILFRED OWEN	Garmon Rhys
SISTER ROGERS	Lindy Whiteford

Director	Simon Godwin
Designer	Alex Eales
Lighting Designer	Lee Curran
Sound Designer	George Dennis
Music	Stuart Earl
Movement Director	Struan Leslie
Assistant Director	Alice Hamilton
Casting Director	Ginny Schiller CDG

Produced by the Touring Consortium Theatre Company and Northampton Royal & Derngate.

The production subsequently toured to York Theatre Royal; King's Theatre, Edinburgh; Alhambra Theatre, Bradford; Theatre Royal, Nottingham; Everyman Theatre, Cheltenham; Richmond Theatre; Wolverhampton Grand Theatre; Darlington Civic Theatre; Oxford Playhouse and Grand Theatre, Blackpool.

Characters

CAPTAIN RIVERS, *anthropologist and physician, fifty-three*
SISTER ROGERS, *a nurse*
SIEGFRIED SASSOON, *soldier and poet, thirty*
SECOND-LIEUTENANT BILLY PRIOR, *soldier and patient,*
    twenty-two
ROBERT GRAVES, *soldier and poet, twenty-two*
MAJOR CAMPBELL, *soldier and patient*
CAPTAIN BURNS, *soldier and patient*
CAPTAIN ANDERSON, *soldier and patient*
MAJOR WILLARD, *soldier and patient*
WILFRED OWEN, *soldier and poet, twenty-four*
LIEUTENANT EVANS
DR YEALLAND, *medical officer*
CALLAN, *a shell-shocked soldier*

And MEDICAL OFFICERS, PATIENTS *and* WAITERS

Place

Craiglockhart Army Hospital, Scotland, and elsewhere.

Time

Summer 1917 to January 1919.

*This text went to press before the end of rehearsals and so may
differ slightly from the play as performed.*

ACT ONE

Craiglockhart Army Hospital, Scotland. It's late at night.
CAPTAIN RIVERS, *a medical officer in his fifties, is at his desk,*
looking through the day's post. He picks up a paperknife and
opens an envelope. Reads a bit of the letter. Puts it on one side.
It's late, he's exhausted and he feels that he can't take any more.

SISTER ROGERS *appears at his side. She's Scottish and*
strong-minded.

SISTER ROGERS. Captain Rivers?

He stares at her, a bit bemused.

Captain Rivers?

RIVERS. Yes?

SISTER ROGERS. Second-Lieutenant Prior has woken up. You
can see him now, if it's not too late for you.

RIVERS. Thank you, Sister Rogers. I'll come at once.

He stands and leaves with her.

*

SIEGFRIED SASSOON – *thirty years old, poised, fit,*
handsome – stands before a medical board of six uniformed
MEDICAL OFFICERS.

MEDICAL OFFICER ONE. Lieutenant Sassoon, you may
proceed.

SIEGFRIED *reads from a document. He's confident and*
assured.

SIEGFRIED. 'I am making this statement as an act of wilful
defiance of military authority, because I believe the war is
being deliberately prolonged by those who have the power to
end it.'

MEDICAL OFFICER TWO (*interrupts irascibly*). May I ask, is this a public statement, or is it purely for the benefit of his commanding officer?

MEDICAL OFFICER THREE. It appears that he has sent copies to a large number of friends and colleagues.

MEDICAL OFFICER FOUR. *And* to the newspapers.

MEDICAL OFFICER THREE. *And* to Mr Hastings Lees-Smith, MP, who intends to raise it in the House of Commons, thereby causing the maximum of embarrassment.

MEDICAL OFFICER FOUR. Which is no doubt the entire intention.

MEDICAL OFFICER ONE. May we go on?

On a nod from the MEDICAL OFFICER, SIEGFRIED *reads.*

SIEGFRIED. 'I am a soldier, convinced that I am acting on behalf of soldiers. I believe that this war, upon which I entered as a war of defence and liberation, has now become a war of aggression and conquest.

'I have seen and endured the suffering of the troops, and I can no longer be a party to prolong these sufferings for ends that I believe to be evil and unjust.

'I am not...'

MEDICAL OFFICER THREE *interrupts.*

MEDICAL OFFICER THREE. Can someone explain to me how this man's refusal to fight is any different from that of a common deserter?

MEDICAL OFFICER ONE. Surely that is a little harsh? The man is mentally ill.

MEDICAL OFFICER TWO. He's been suffering from hallucinations.

MEDICAL OFFICER THREE. Only according to Captain Graves.

MEDICAL OFFICER FOUR. Well, that won't wash. Graves is his friend. He's covering up for him. Isn't that obvious?

MEDICAL OFFICER ONE. I ought to point out that the doctor's report agrees with Lieutenant Graves in every respect. Lieutenant Sassoon…

SIEGFRIED. Sir?

MEDICAL OFFICER ONE. You will recuse yourself while we deliberate.

*

In a small pool of light we see BILLY PRIOR, *in bed but awake.* BILLY *is twenty-two, skinny and tough with the hunched posture and strong chest of an asthmatic.* SISTER ROGERS *and* RIVERS *come in.*

SISTER ROGERS. Mr Prior? Your new doctor is here to see you. Sit up and pay attention, if you please.

No response. Irritated, she straightens his pillow and sheets. RIVERS *has a slight stammer.*

RIVERS. Good evening, Mr Prior.

BILLY *stares back at him and their eyes meet. There's silence for a moment.*

SISTER ROGERS. It's no use staring at the doctor like that. He's here to help you, if he can.

RIVERS. Has he spoken at all since he arrived?

SISTER ROGERS. Not one word. Dr Brock couldn't get anywhere with him.

RIVERS. Yes, he told me. Could you bring me a teaspoon?

SISTER ROGERS. Certainly, doctor.

She goes. RIVERS *sits by the bed.*

RIVERS (*to* BILLY). How have you been you sleeping, Mr Prior?

BILLY *shrugs elaborately.*

Have you been having nightmares?

BILLY *shrugs again, as in 'Maybe'.*

What are they about?

BILLY *takes a notepad and pencil from the side of the bed, scrawls an answer ('I DON'T REMEMBER') and hands over the pad.* RIVERS *reads it.*

Can you not remember at *all*? It's characteristic of nightmares, you know, that one *does* remember them.

SISTER ROGERS *comes in with a teaspoon.*

(*To her.*) Does he talk in his sleep?

BILLY *frowns, worried.*

SISTER ROGERS. Just bits and bobs. Nothing one can make any sense of.

RIVERS *takes the teaspoon.*

RIVERS. Thank you.

(*To* BILLY.) I'm going to take a quick look at the back of your throat. Open wide.

BILLY *opens his mouth, and* RIVERS *inserts the teaspoon and draws it firmly across the back of* BILLY*'s throat.* BILLY *chokes and protests, trying to push* RIVERS*'s hand away.*

(*To* SISTER ROGERS.) There's no area of analgesia.

BILLY *snatches the notepad and scrawls on it:* (*'THAT HURT'*).

(*Reads.*) It didn't *really* hurt though, did it? It might have been a touch uncomfortable.

BILLY *spreads his arms wonderingly as in 'How would you know?'* RIVERS *hands the teaspoon back to* SISTER ROGERS.

Thank you, sister.

(*To* BILLY.) I have to tell you, Mr Prior, that this hospital has not yet received your records from your regiment.

BILLY *signals: 'So what?'*

No, it's more serious than that. If I'm to find out what caused you to be like this, I'll need to know what happened to you. Do you understand me?

SISTER ROGERS. He understands all right.

RIVERS. There's nothing physically wrong with you, so I can't cure you by sticking a needle into you, or giving you electric shocks. I have to get into your mind. So I need a doorway. I need to know where you were and what you were doing when the trouble started. And at present I know nothing whatsoever.

SISTER ROGERS. You're a man of mystery.

RIVERS. So… if your regiment doesn't send me the information that I need, you'll have to tell me yourself. If you want to get well.

BILLY *scribbles on the notepad and hands it to* SISTER ROGERS. *She reads.*

(*To her.*) What did he write this time?

SISTER ROGERS. 'No more words.'

*

Craiglockhart. Summer, day. SIEGFRIED *and his friend* ROBERT GRAVES *look at the façade of Craiglockhart: once a Victorian 'hydro' hotel, now a military hospital.*

SIEGFRIED. God, how depressing.

GRAVES. It's not very cheerful.

SIEGFRIED. It's like a bloody mausoleum.

GRAVES. Or the sort of hotel one might retire to in order to cut one's throat. Look, there's a patient over there.

They look.

Am I imagining this, or is he walking in a rather peculiar way?

SIEGFRIED. Lurching from side to side.

GRAVES. He probably thinks he's dodging a German sniper.

SIEGFRIED. What else do you expect in a loony bin?

GRAVES. Come on, it isn't all bad. There's a couple playing tennis.

SIEGFRIED. Where?

GRAVES. There, over that hedge. Can't you hear them?

They listen to the distant sound of pok-pok-pok.

I saw a golf course out of the taxi window. Cheer up, Sass.
You won't have too bad a time.

SIEGFRIED. It's the humiliation. That's the devil of it.

SISTER ROGERS *appears.*

SISTER ROGERS (*to* GRAVES). Lieutenant Sassoon?

GRAVES. *That* is Lieutenant Sassoon. I'm Captain Graves. I'm
his military escort.

SISTER ROGERS. Will you be staying the night, Captain
Graves?

GRAVES. I will, and I'm taking the 8.20 express from
Waverley Station in the morning.

SISTER ROGERS. I'll see that your bed's made up. This is
your key. Will you look after it, please?

She gives GRAVES *a key.*

(*To* SIEGFRIED.) Welcome to Craiglockhart, Mr Sassoon.
You will be sleeping in room number eighty-four. As you are
a patient, you will not have a key. Will you follow me
please? Captain Rivers is waiting for you.

SIEGFRIED *follows her to* RIVERS*'s consulting room,
leaving* GRAVES *behind and soon out of sight.*

*

RIVERS*'s consulting room.* RIVERS *is at work, intent as
always on whatever he's doing.* SIEGFRIED *appears.*

SIEGFRIED. Captain Rivers?

RIVERS *looks up.*

RIVERS. Come in. Take a seat.

SIEGFRIED *does.*

I shall be overseeing your recovery while you're here. I am a
physician and a psychologist of the, ah, the Freudian school.
Do you know anything of the work of Dr Freud?

SIEGFRIED. I've read *The Interpretation of Dreams*.

RIVERS. In German?

SIEGFRIED. Obviously in German. I didn't know it'd been translated.

RIVERS. It hasn't. Good, we shall have much to talk about.

He continues, looking at SIEGFRIED *intently, as doctors do on a first meeting.*

I believe Captain Graves escorted you here?

SIEGFRIED. Yes, he's been doing a lot of running about on my account. You've no idea how hard he had to work in order to rig the medical board.

RIVERS. I don't want to sound priggish, but the idea that a medical board was *rigged* is highly disagreeable to me.

SIEGFRIED. It was just a matter of persuading them that I was mad. I wouldn't have argued that myself. I'd rather have done it the straight way and been court-martialled, but apparently a court martial was out of the question.

RIVERS. Who told you that? Was it Graves?

SIEGFRIED. How did you know?

RIVERS. Why did he think it was out of the question?

SIEGFRIED. He said the last thing the War Office wanted was to give me a public platform to spout my views.

RIVERS. Meaning the views that you stated in your Declaration?

SIEGFRIED. Exactly those.

RIVERS *opens a file and looks at it.*

RIVERS. So you refused to obey your orders?

SIEGFRIED. Yes I did.

RIVERS *takes off his spectacles and stares at* SIEGFRIED.

RIVERS. You realise that men have been shot for less?

SIEGFRIED. If the War Office had *wanted* to shoot me, they could have done so ten times over. But they preferred to hush me up by pretending I'd had a breakdown.

RIVERS. Well, I shall disregard the politics and treat you like any other patient.

SIEGFRIED. Please do.

RIVERS. What sort of thing did the medical board ask you?

SIEGFRIED. Don't you know?

RIVERS. I'd rather hear it from you.

SIEGFRIED. They wanted to know if I objected to fighting on religious grounds. I said I didn't have a religion. They asked if I was qualified to decide when the war should end? I said, no, I wasn't.

RIVERS. What else?

SIEGFRIED. How about this:

He laughs.

'Captain Graves tells us that you were first-rate at throwing bombs at the Germans. Do you still hate the Germans?'

RIVERS. What did you say?

SIEGFRIED. I said that yes, I'm pretty good with a grenade. And no, I don't still hate the Germans.

RIVERS. But you used to?

SIEGFRIED. Briefly, yes. A friend of mine had been killed, so I used to go out into no man's land every night, looking for Huns to kill. Or giving them a chance to kill me. I was pretty indifferent either way.

RIVERS. Is that where you got your nickname?

SIEGFRIED. Which one?

RIVERS. 'Mad Jack'. You know that taking pointless risks is one of the first signs of a war neurosis?

SIEGFRIED. No, I didn't know that.

RIVERS. Nightmares and hallucinations come later.

He looks in SIEGFRIED's *file.*

Tell me about yours.

SIEGFRIED. I had a few nightmares when I got back from France. They've mostly stopped.

RIVERS. What about your hallucinations?

SIEGFRIED. Graves really *did* talk to the medical board, didn't he?

RIVERS waits.

Well… when I woke up from a nightmare, the images didn't stop. I'd see…

RIVERS continues to wait, listens.

Corpses. Men with half their faces shot off, crawling across the floor. I'd been to my club for lunch, and I nodded off on a bench, and suddenly the pavement of Piccadilly was covered in rotting bodies. People were treading on their faces.

RIVERS. Did you think you were going mad?

SIEGFRIED. No, because all the time that this was happening, I managed to write one or two rather good poems.

RIVERS. You don't think it's possible for a person who's mad to write a good poem?

SIEGFRIED. No, I don't.

RIVERS. That's very interesting.

He takes a couple of papers out of a folder.

These are some of your poems, I assume?

SIEGFRIED is put out.

SIEGFRIED. How did they get there?

RIVERS. Graves again, I imagine.

(Reads.) 'Blighters'.

Holding a poem, he looks up at SIEGFRIED.

Could you read it to me? I'm no judge of poetry, but it might be helpful from the psychological point of view.

He hands over the paper. SIEGFRIED *takes it and reads.*

SIEGFRIED.

>'The House is crammed: tier beyond tier they grin
>And cackle at the Show, while prancing ranks
>Of harlots shrill the chorus, drunk with din;
>"We're sure the Kaiser loves our dear old Tanks!"

He continues to read with increasing savagery.

>I'd like to see a Tank come down the stalls,
>Lurching to rag-time tunes, or "Home Sweet Home",
>And there'd be no more jokes in Music Halls
>To mock the riddled corpses round Bapaume.'

RIVERS. You're saying you'd like to see the audience crushed to a bloody pulp?

SIEGFRIED. Yes, I would.

RIVERS. Why?

SIEGFRIED. For treating the war as a piece of cheap entertainment.

RIVERS. So you hate civilians? Or is 'hate' too strong a word?

SIEGFRIED. No, it's not.

RIVERS. I see.

He takes back the poem and closes the file.

Have you thought about what you'll do, while you're here?

SIEGFRIED. Go for walks, read.

RIVERS. Will you be able to write? I hope you will, but we can't give you a room of your own.

SIEGFRIED. I'll write if I have to sit on the roof.

RIVERS. About your war experiences?

SIEGFRIED. Yes, of course.

RIVERS. Very good. We run a progressive regime here. There's a rambling club, a dramatic society, a swimming pool. You can go into town whenever you want to. I'll sign you into the Conservative Club, if that appeals to you. And I shall see you on Tuesdays, Fridays and Sundays, at…

He looks.

…eight-thirty after dinner.

SIEGFRIED. Do you think I'm mad?

RIVERS. No, I don't. I don't even think you've got a war neurosis.

SIEGFRIED. What *have* I got?

RIVERS. You seem to me to have an extremely powerful *anti-war* neurosis.

He smiles at his own joke and stands, prior to ending the interview.

You realise, don't you, that it's my job to alter your complete way of thinking?

SIEGFRIED. What do you mean?

RIVERS. I can't be neutral, in the way that psychoanalysts are meant to be. Dr Freud would try to convert your neuroses into normal human unhappiness, or something equally abstract. My task is different. You're in excellent physical condition and you're not insane, so it's my duty to get you back into active service as soon as I can. Good morning.

SIEGFRIED. Good morning.

SIEGFRIED goes. There is a wire recorder on RIVERS's desk. He turns it on.

RIVERS (*dictates*). The patient is…

There's a knock at the door.

Yes?

GRAVES *looks in.*

GRAVES. You wanted to see me?

RIVERS. Yes, come in.

GRAVES comes in and spies a statuette.

GRAVES. Ah, Laocoön. The priest who warned the Trojans against the wooden horse. The image is sometimes thought to depict man on the one hand fighting the world around him and, on the other hand, fighting himself.

RIVERS. That's why I keep it there. Would you mind putting it down?

GRAVES *does*.

You seem to have done a certain amount of manipulation behind the scenes.

GRAVES. Well, I had to. Sass is a very good chap, but he's a bit of a chump at times. And now he'd got himself within an inch of being court-martialled. Well, fortunately, I have some pull at the War Office, so I took a trip to Whitehall and I managed to cool them down.

RIVERS. By saying that he was having a mental breakdown?

GRAVES. Exactly that. And then I persuaded Sass to play along with the nonsense, which was uphill work, I can assure you.

RIVERS. How did you talk him round?

GRAVES. I lied.

RIVERS. I thought you probably had.

GRAVES. I swore by all that I hold most sacred that a court martial simply wasn't on the cards. It left me feeling a little bit sticky, I must confess, but… I say, I didn't do wrong, did I?

RIVERS. I think you did the best you could for your friend. As you saw it. Thank you, Lieutenant.

*

That evening. We're at a table in the dining hall. The sounds of a crowd of men. SIEGFRIED *and* GRAVES *have just joined a bluff, anxious officer with a tic. His name is* CAMPBELL. *Also a very thin, silent, tragic-looking officer named* BURNS, *and an older, cheerful officer without a tic and reasonably normal-looking: this is* CAPTAIN ANDERSON. *Bowls of soup are before them.*

ANDERSON. Oh, will you be joining us? Excellent, excellent. I am Rafe Anderson, medical officer as was with the Royal Flying Corps.

CAMPBELL. I'm Jim Campbell. Glad to make your acquaintance. I only wish it was in happier circumstances. The grub here isn't up to much. You'd do better to eat in town, if it weren't so pricey.

ANDERSON (*indicates the man sitting at the end of the table*). That's Tom Burns. (*Whispers*.) He won't be talking.

GRAVES *introduces himself to the company*.

GRAVES. Robert Graves, First Battalion, 'A' Company, Royal Welch Fusiliers. This is my friend Sassoon of 'C' Company.

CAMPBELL. *Siegfried* Sassoon?

SIEGFRIED. That's me.

GRAVES (*to* SIEGFRIED). It sounds as though this officer has read your book.

CAMPBELL. His *book*? I've never heard of it. But I saw your name, Sassoon, among today's announcements. You and I will be sharing a room, it seems. I have to say, your name is an odd one. How did *that* come about?

SIEGFRIED. 'Sassoon' is an old Sephardic name.

CAMPBELL. No, the other one! Who the *devil* would saddle their son with a name like *Siegfried*?

SIEGFRIED. My parents did, if you put it like that. It isn't my fault.

CAMPBELL (*with heavy irony*). That's one way of looking at it, I suppose. But I can think of another one.

He rises, with distaste:

Excuse me, gentlemen. I have a conversation pending over there.

He moves to the other end of the table.

ANDERSON (*quietly*). He means no harm. He has a bee in his bonnet about the Germans. Not a bad bee to have in wartime, mind you. Do you play golf?

SIEGFRIED. I do.

ANDERSON. What's your handicap?

SIEGFRIED. Ten.

ANDERSON. Ah, then we might have a game!

SIEGFRIED. I'm afraid I haven't brought my clubs.

ANDERSON. Send for them, send for them. Some of the best courses in the country round here. I would be out on the links tomorrow, only my wife decided to pay me a visit. All very well, except she's cancelled at the last minute.

CAMPBELL (*gloomily*). Brown Windsor again, gentlemen.

Taking this as the signal to start, all except for BURNS *begin to eat.* ANDERSON *murmurs, with a sideways glance at* BURNS.

ANDERSON. I do hope dinner will pass without incident.

GRAVES. Why shouldn't it?

ANDERSON. We'll see, we'll see. How are you feeling, Captain Burns? Any better today?

BURNS *nods doubtfully. As* ANDERSON *watches with apprehension, he takes a spoonful of soup and, very cautiously, another.*

Then he vomits. It's a slow and painful business, as he has eaten nothing for weeks. His vomiting and his helplessness awaken in each man a traumatic memory of conflict, and that memory is what we now see. The light dims down to that of a moonlit night, and the loud rumble of shellfire is heard. BURNS *clings for support to the man nearest to him, whose response, like that of the other men at the table, is as if he had been injured in battle: they hold him, comfort him and mop the mess as though it were an outpouring of blood. All available men are involved.*

SISTER ROGERS *appears at the table.*

SISTER ROGERS (*very gently*). Captain Burns, will you come with me? There's nothing to worry about. Hold on to my arm.

BURNS, *miserable and humiliated, allows himself to be led out and the scene returns to everyday.* ANDERSON *murmurs to* SIEGFRIED *and* GRAVES:

ANDERSON. He was blown up into the air, you see, and when he came round, his face was deep in the guts of a dead German. His mouth was full of the rotten filth. Now he can't hold anything down. Terrible, terrible.

*

Night. RIVERS*'s consulting room. His recording device is running and he is dictating his notes into it.*

RIVERS. We lead Burns to his room.
   Put him to bed.
   The smell of vomit on his breath.
   His misery at upsetting the other officers.
   I glimpse the man that he used to be.
   That's the most distressing part of it.
   I put an arm around him.
   I murmur, 'It doesn't get any better, does it?'
   He shakes his head.
   It's a strange kind of healing I do, getting men well enough to go back to a place where such vile things can happen to them.
   The ambiguity of my job.

He unscrews a bottle of whisky, pours himself a restrained measure and sips. He's not a drunk. Looks at his watch. Listens.

2 a.m.
   Uncanny atmosphere as always late at night.
   Half-heard screams and mutterings.
   Men lying panic-stricken in their beds.
   Or roaming the corridors like ghosts.
   One of them said to me, 'It's like being in the trenches without any sky.'

There's a brisk knock on the door. RIVERS *calls:*

No, whatever it is, no.

SISTER ROGERS *appears and he pauses his recording device.*

SISTER ROGERS. Excuse me, Captain Rivers, I saw your light on. It's Prior again. He started shouting in his sleep and he woke himself up. And now he's talking.

RIVERS. Will he go back to sleep?

SISTER ROGERS. Oh yes, I think so.

RIVERS. Tell him I'll see him in the morning. Thank you, Sister Rogers.

SISTER ROGERS. Will you not go to bed now? It's awful late. You look worn out.

RIVERS. I am. I mean, I will. Goodnight.

She goes. He turns on his recording device. Poised to speak into it, he says nothing.

*

The sickbay. Morning. BILLY *is in an iron bedstead.* RIVERS *grabs a chair and sits beside the bed.*

RIVERS. I'm very glad the trouble's over.

BILLY *has a northern accent.*

BILLY. Well, the *voiceless* trouble has. It may come back. It comes and goes.

RIVERS. What brings it on?

BILLY (*dismissive*). When I get upset.

RIVERS. Did it upset you to be sent here?

BILLY. It did in a way. I don't like Edinburgh. It's all old ladies and knitted jumpers.

RIVERS *gets out a notebook and pencil.*

RIVERS. What did you do before the war?

BILLY. I was a clerk in a shipping office.

RIVERS. Did you like it?

BILLY. No. What did *you* do?

RIVERS *registers the prickliness but ignores it.*

RIVERS. I did medical research and teaching. I've also practised social anthropology.

BILLY. Did *you* like *that*?

RIVERS. Yes, very much. Can we get back to you? When you were first commissioned, how did you fit in with the others?

BILLY. Are you asking how a man from a Bradford backstreet became an officer?

RIVERS. No, obviously the composition of the officer class will change if there've been a lot of casualties. Did you experience any snobbery?

BILLY. Look, it's obvious when you arrive that some people are more welcome than others. It helps if you've been to the right school, it helps if you hold your knife and fork in a particular way. And there's your seat on a horse. Oh yes! They make you ride round and round this bloody ring with your fingers behind your head. No stirrups or saddle. I found that most enlightening. I realised that somewhere at the back of their *tiny* minds they really do think the war will end in an almighty *cavalry charge*. The military mind doesn't change much, does it?

RIVERS. How *was* your seat on a horse?

BILLY. Sticky. No, that's *good*. It means you don't fall off. So that was *something* in my favour. It drives me crazy when people say that everyone's equal at the front. It's just not true. There's inequality through and through, like it were stamped in a stick of rock. I'll tell you the worst thing. I used to sit in this café in France, and just across the road there was a brothel with a queue outside. The privates, the men, were allowed two minutes each in there.

RIVERS. How long did the officers get?

BILLY. More than the men. That's all I know. I've never paid for it and I don't intend to.

RIVERS *opens a file on his lap*.

Ask away.

RIVERS. On the 29th of April, you were brought to the 13th Casualty Clearing Station and diagnosed as neurasthenic, meaning 'shell-shocked'.

BILLY. I know what it means.

RIVERS. And it was noted that you suffered from mutism.

BILLY. 'Couldn't talk.'

RIVERS. Which is unusual amongst officers. Do you have any other recurring problems?

BILLY. Headaches.

RIVERS. What about your breathing?

BILLY. What about it?

RIVERS. You're asthmatic.

BILLY. It doesn't affect my fighting ability.

RIVERS. We can talk about that later.

He closes the file and puts it down.

The file ends there.

BILLY. How very sad.

RIVERS. Who was it who brought you to the Casualty Station?

BILLY. I don't know and I don't want to. All this talking doesn't *help*. It churns things up and makes them real.

RIVERS. But they *are* real. Aren't they?

BILLY. All I can say is that I'd rather talk to a real human being than a strip of empathetic wallpaper.

RIVERS *stands*.

RIVERS. I can't help you if you don't want to get better. Good day.

BILLY. Oy! You can't just walk out on me like that!

RIVERS. Mr Prior, there are a hundred and sixty-eight sick officers in this hospital, and they need attention just as much as you do. Good morning.

BILLY. It's not fair to say I don't want to get better.

RIVERS. But you won't cooperate with the treatment.

BILLY. I don't *agree* with the treatment. Why has it got to be like this? All the questions from *you*, all the answers from *me*. Why can't it be both ways?

RIVERS. If you went to the doctor with bronchitis and he spent half of the session telling you about his lumbago, wouldn't you think he was an idiot?

BILLY. Yes, but if I went to my doctor *in despair* it might help if he knew the *meaning* of the word.

RIVERS. *Are* you in despair?

BILLY *sighs, ostentatiously impatient.*

People who are in despair don't *care* what the doctor thinks. That's the whole point about despair. Shall we try once more?

BILLY. Can we go on to the balcony? It's stuffy in here.

RIVERS. Yes, if you like.

BILLY *sits up, puts on his dressing gown and slippers and they move forward into brighter light. There are a couple of basket chairs. It's a sunny, warm day in August. A game of cricket is heard intermittently from below: not a formal match, just an impromptu knock-up.* BILLY *gets out tobacco and papers and rolls a cigarette.*

That isn't a good idea with asthma.

BILLY. You think that smoking might shorten my life? Do you know how long the average officer lasts in France?

RIVERS. Three months. You're not in France. What is the last thing that you *do* remember?

BILLY (*replies unwillingly*). We moved up to the line, and we attacked at dawn the next morning.

RIVERS. What do you remember about the attack?

BILLY. It were just like any other attack.

RIVERS *waits.* BILLY *takes a puff of his fag.*

All right. You wait, you try to calm down anybody who's having the shits or who's about to throw up. You cross fingers that you won't do either of those things yourself. You start the countdown. You blow the whistle. You climb the ladder. You wriggle through a gap in the wire, lie flat, wait for everybody else to get out… those that are left, there's already quite a few been hit... and then you stand up. And you start walking. *Not* at the double. Straight line. Open country. Broad daylight. You're walking towards a line of machine guns. And you're being shelled at all the way.

RIVERS. What did you feel?

BILLY. What does it matter what I *felt*?

RIVERS. You describe it as though it were a slightly absurd event in somebody else's life.

BILLY. *Slightly* absurd?

RIVERS. *Extremely* absurd. You'd need to be inhuman to be as detached as that.

BILLY. All right, I'll tell you. It felt sexy.

RIVERS. What?

BILLY. You know those men who lurk around in bushes waiting to jump out on unsuspecting ladies and show what they've got? It felt like that. Like I *imagine* it feels.

RIVERS. Was that all you felt?

BILLY. You keep up a kind of chanting. 'Not so fast!' 'Steady on the left!' I look round after me and the ground is covered in wounded men. Writhing, lying on top of each other, like fish in a pond that's drying out. I feel this...

RIVERS *waits*.

I feel this burst of exultation. Then there's a shell on its way, and the next thing I'm in the air... *fluttering* down.

He demonstrates with a hand.

I came to in a crater with half a dozen of the men. I thought I was paralysed, but I got to my feet. I told them to fish the brandy out of my pocket and we passed it round. Then a feller appeared on the rim of the crater and, instead of crawling down, he put his hands to his sides and he slid down on his backside. The rest of us laughed like...

He censors out 'fuck'.

...like nobody's business.

He smiles at the memory.

We waited till dark and then we made a rush back to the line. That's all I remember.

RIVERS. Do you have a theory about what might have happened afterwards?

BILLY *replies with furious antagonism.*

BILLY. *I don't remember.* And I *don't* have a theory. *Nothing.*

RIVERS *closes his file.*

RIVERS. One of the nurses will turf you out of bed this evening. I'll see you tomorrow at 9 a.m.

He leaves.

*

On his way from the sickbay, RIVERS *is accosted by* MAJOR WILLARD, *propelling himself in a wheelchair.*

WILLARD. Captain Rivers! I insist that you move that young man out of the sickbay.

RIVERS. Who, Prior?

WILLARD. Yes, Prior! None of us got a wink of sleep last night. He was screaming as though all the devils of hell were after him!

RIVERS. They probably were. Frankly, Major Willard, he has a lot more reason to be in the sickbay than you do.

WILLARD. Me? What are you talking about? I've broken my spine! I'm paralysed! The massage is useless!

RIVERS. There's nothing wrong with your spine.

WILLARD. I see, I see! You think I'm malingering, don't you! You think I'm swinging the lead!

RIVERS. I know you're not.

WILLARD. But you're accusing me of being a coward!

RIVERS. Not at all. Paralysis is no use to a coward. He needs his legs to run away. You refuse to run away, but you're a sensible man who doesn't want to be killed. You've found an answer to that dilemma. Now go back in there and be a good friend to Prior. He needs it.

With a 'hmh!' of annoyance, WILLARD *spins round in his wheelchair and leaves.*

*

The grounds. It's still sunny and warm. SIEGFRIED *is reading* The Times. RIVERS *arrives.* SIEGFRIED *looks up.*

SIEGFRIED. You'll be pleased to know that I've hit the headlines.

RIVERS. Where, in *The Times*?

SIEGFRIED. Where else? In fact it's rather a modest mention. Parliamentary Report. Mr Hastings Lees-Smith MP asked a question, and the Minister replied that the unnamed officer concerned is suffering from a nervous breakdown. No further action to be taken. So much for my glorious martyrdom.

RIVERS. What did you expect?

SIEGFRIED. Oh, I don't know.

He's about to stand.

RIVERS. Don't get up. We can talk out here. It's a shame to waste the summer.

SIEGFRIED *stands, unbuckles his Sam Browne.*

SIEGFRIED. Then I'll strip down a bit.

RIVERS. You can't do that. You know the rules.

SIEGFRIED. Oh, what drivel.

He takes off his tunic, undoes the top buttons of his shirt. RIVERS *takes out a notebook. While this is going on:*

RIVERS. I'd like to start by asking you about your family.

SIEGFRIED. What for?

RIVERS. It's part of the process.

SIEGFRIED. Oh, all right.

RIVERS. Tell me about your mother.

SIEGFRIED. Imperious. Proud. Adoring.

RIVERS. Your father?

SIEGFRIED. My father died when I was eight, and I hadn't seen much of him even before that. He left home when I was five.

RIVERS. Do you remember him?

SIEGFRIED. His moustache used to tickle me when he kissed me. I was too young to go to his funeral, which was just as well, because my brother was terrified by it.

RIVERS. Why?

SIEGFRIED. It was a Jewish funeral. He said it was full of old men with long beards and funny hats going jabber-jabber-jabber.

RIVERS. What difference do you think it would have made to you if he had lived?

SIEGFRIED *considers this*.

SIEGFRIED. Maybe I wouldn't have felt so split-up.

RIVERS. Meaning what?

SIEGFRIED. Just that all through school and Cambridge… and after that just messing about, I've always felt… in a way… that I was three different people.

RIVERS (*non-committal*). Mm-hm.

SIEGFRIED. There's the riding, hunting, cricketing 'me', and there's the 'me' who writes poetry and loves music.

RIVERS. What's the third one?

SIEGFRIED. I'm sorry?

RIVERS. You said three.

SIEGFRIED. Did I? I meant two. (*With sarcasm*.) I suppose Dr Freud would say that I deliberately left one out.

RIVERS. Not… deliberately. It must have been stressful for you, being so divided.

SIEGFRIED. Yes, it was. I didn't seem able to feel any of the... the things that one is supposed to feel.

RIVERS. Mm-hm.

SIEGFRIED. I'd be unable to sleep at night. I'd wait until the house was quiet and then just get up and, and walk about.

RIVERS. Was there anywhere at all where you felt comfortable?

SIEGFRIED. Just the army. That's the only place I've ever really belonged.

RIVERS. Was there anything else that helped?

SIEGFRIED. Yes, there was. I, I read a book by a man called Edward Carpenter. It's called *The Intermediate Sex*. Have you, have you heard of it?

RIVERS *registers this unexpected near-confession.*

RIVERS. I've read it. How did it help you?

SIEGFRIED. I saw that there were, there were other people like me, who had... similar feelings. That I wasn't a freak. So I wrote to Carpenter and I went up to Chesterfield to see him and his, his friend. What do you think of the book?

RIVERS. I admire the courage of it. But I don't know if his concept of an intermediate sex is a helpful one. You are not *neuter*, and neither am I, however unorthodox our desires may be.

SIEGFRIED *notes these last few words.*

Carpenter is a pacifist, isn't he? Was he an influence on your Declaration?

SIEGFRIED. What influenced me was my experience at the front. I can make up my own mind.

RIVERS. I'm sure you can. Have you met other pacifists?

SIEGFRIED. Bertrand Russell. Oh, and there's a writer, Robert Ross. I didn't show him my Declaration. He would have run a mile from it.

RIVERS. Why?

SIEGFRIED. He was a friend of Oscar Wilde's. He keeps his head down.

RIVERS. And you? Do you keep your head down?

SIEGFRIED. No, I hold it up as high as it will go.

RIVERS. You don't like safety, do you?

SIEGFRIED. I despise it.

RIVERS. Well, you've got… nearly three months of safety here until your case is reviewed. *At least*. If you carry on refusing to serve, you'll be safe for the rest of the war.

SIEGFRIED. What's your point?

RIVERS. Don't you think you might find it difficult being safe, while men are dying in France?

SIEGFRIED *flares up*.

SIEGFRIED. I'll just have to learn to live with it, won't I? Because nobody else in this *stinking* country seems to find it difficult. And you can stop trying to get me to change my mind. It isn't working.

RIVERS. Then let me give you some advice. Ross's caution about… revealing his nature… may seem excessive to you, or even cowardly. But don't dismiss it out of hand. One's inclinations could be used against one to discredit one's views. I'd hate to see that happening to you.

SIEGFRIED. I thought discrediting my views is what *you're* trying to do.

RIVERS. Let's say, I'm fussy about the methods.

WILLARD *wheels over to them, still very annoyed*.

WILLARD. Sassoon, this is most improper. 'No officer may appear in public with any garment missing.' Go indoors and replace your tunic and belt *at once*.

SIEGFRIED. What a ridiculous place this is!

WILLARD *wheels off as* SIEGFRIED *goes indoors*. RIVERS *is accosted en route by* CAMPBELL, *who is twitching more than when seen before*.

CAMPBELL. Ah, Captain Rivers, just the man!

RIVERS. Major Campbell?

CAMPBELL. That young officer – (*Twitch, twitch.*) you've just been talking to.

RIVERS. Sassoon?

CAMPBELL. That's right, Sassoon. (*Twitch.*) You know I'm – (*Twitch, twitch.*) I'm sharing a room with him.

RIVERS. Do you object to that?

CAMPBELL. Hm, yes, I very much might do.

RIVERS. Would you mind telling me why?

CAMPBELL *looks around furtively, before saying quietly:*

CAMPBELL. Well, it's somewhat embarrassing to say this, but I think he might be a… (*Twitch.*)

Pause.

RIVERS. A what?

CAMPBELL. Don't force me to spell it out. You know what I mean.

RIVERS. No, I don't.

CAMPBELL (*furtively*). A German spy.

RIVERS (*with relief*). Oh, no, I'm certain he's not! German spies *never* call themselves 'Siegfried'.

CAMPBELL *looks astonished.*

CAMPBELL. No more they do. Hadn't thought about it like that. (*Twitch.*)

He pats RIVERS *on the shoulder.*

Thank you for putting my mind at rest. Just thought I'd mention it.

He goes.

*

A pub in Edinburgh. BILLY *is at the bar, rolling a cigarette. We hear the voices of other drinkers, especially that of a group of young Scots women bantering and laughing.*

BILLY *lights his fag and looks over at them without much interest. He turns and sees* WILFRED OWEN *at the bar.* WILFRED *is twenty-four, not tall, with a warm voice and a slight stammer. He wears a distinguishing 'Craiglockhart' armband.*

BILLY. I know you.

WILFRED. Do you?

BILLY. Yes, you're at Craiglockhart. I'm there too.

WILFRED. I've never seen you there.

BILLY. Well, I haven't been there long and I've been in the sickbay half the time.

WILFRED. You look healthy enough.

BILLY. I am. I got a bit of a problem with my chest, that's all.

WILFRED. Because of the fighting?

BILLY. No, I've always had it.

WILFRED. That's too bad.

BILLY. It's nowt to worry about.

They drink.

WILFRED. I didn't think you could be a patient there because you're not wearing an armband.

BILLY. It's in my pocket.

He takes it out of his pocket and shows it.

I'm on the prowl. Nubile young ladies tend to be put off by obvious signs of madness. Haven't you noticed that?

WILFRED. Not really, no. I haven't had the chance, I suppose. Oh, I'm Owen.

BILLY. I'm Prior, Billy Prior. What're you doing in Edinburgh, if you're not looking for a girl?

WILFRED. It's my doctor's idea. Dr Brock. He has us trudging up and down the Mound making notes, or climbing up the Outlook Tower or going on rambles. It's all about restoring our relationship with the material world.

BILLY. He sounds crackers.

WILFRED. I think he's good. Who's *your* doctor?

BILLY. I suffer from the abominable Captain Rivers.

WILFRED. What's abominable about him?

BILLY. He never stops asking questions. On and on. I make it a rule to answer one question every day with a big fat lie.

WILFRED. Does he know you're lying?

BILLY. Oh yes, he's sharp as a box of knives. The other day I told him I couldn't remember something, and he said, quick as a flash, 'Oh well, if you're gonna play games with me, I'm not gonna waste my time, I've got Lieutenant Sassoon waiting for me downstairs.'

WILFRED *stares at him.*

WILFRED. Did you say Sassoon?

BILLY. What of it?

WILFRED. *Siegfried* Sassoon?

BILLY. Search me. Oh, no, I remember now. Major Campbell thought he must be a German spy. That's right, it's Siegfried.

WILFRED. I can't believe it.

BILLY. Why?

WILFRED. He had a book of war poems out last year.

BILLY. What, were they published?

WILFRED. Published, reviewed, the lot. They're the only truthful things about the war that anyone's written. He's a wonderful writer. He's a giant.

BILLY. You should knock on his door and say 'hello'.

WILFRED. I haven't got the nerve. No, not a chance.

They drink. BILLY *looks down the bar.*

BILLY. Do you know that feller?

WILFRED. Which one?

BILLY. That ginger-headed lad over there. He keeps staring at you.

WILFRED looks.

Don't look now. He's leaving anyway.

WILFRED. I never saw him in my life.

The group of Scots girls chatting and laughing can still be heard.

(*To* BILLY.) Didn't you say you were looking for a girl?

BILLY turns and follows WILFRED's eye-line.

BILLY. I saw them lasses before. They're a peculiar colour. They're yellow.

WILFRED. They're not *very* yellow.

BILLY. Their skin is yellow. Even their hair is yellow.

WILFRED. They're munitions girls. They go that colour because of the explosives that they're packing all day. I think it's quite attractive. It's like saffron.

BILLY grins.

BILLY. Besides, it's all the same in the dark.

WILFRED replies as heartily as he can.

WILFRED. You're right about that.

BILLY leaves the bar and goes over towards the girls. WILFRED looks over to where the ginger-haired boy went out, finishes his beer quickly and goes out after him.

*

The golf course. A hot, sunny, August morning. SIEGFRIED *and* ANDERSON *have been held up by the players ahead.*

ANDERSON. My wife was coming for tea this afternoon and now she's cancelled again. Most annoying. Still, it gives me the chance to pick a bone with you.

SIEGFRIED. What's that?

ANDERSON. Tell me, Sassoon, and don't take offence at this…
do you think you're the only person who cares about the war?

SIEGFRIED, *who wasn't expecting this, is startled.*

SIEGFRIED. Why do you imagine that I do?

ANDERSON. I'll tell you. It's that bloody self-righteous
Declaration of yours. As though everyone else except for you
was a callous bastard. Do you think I'm callous? Do you
think Captain Rivers is callous?

SIEGFRIED. No, I don't. I think he cares a great deal. I expect
that you do too.

ANDERSON. Then what the hell were you on about?

SIEGFRIED. It was when I got back to London. I got sick to
death of hearing old gentlemen parroting the lies they'd read
in the newspapers. Or having lunch at The Ritz with
perfectly nice society ladies all prattling about our noble
cause. While men like us, who actually know what we're
talking about, don't say a thing, because we vaguely believe
that it's bad form to tell the truth.

ANDERSON. Well, that's all very fine, old chap, but meanwhile
the Germans are sitting tight in Belgium impaling babies on
their bayonets.

(*With challenge*.) Or is that just another lie?

SIEGFRIED, *keen to avoid a row, looks ahead.*

SIEGFRIED. Look, we can move on.

ANDERSON. Ah, so we can. Well, I appreciate your frankness,
old chap. And it's none of my business anyway. None at all. I
think the niblick, don't you?

*He chooses a club and readies himself. Pauses in order to
calm down.*

Steady the Buffs.

*Apparently calm now, he takes a drive at the ball and
completely misses it, or maybe knocks it a few feeble inches
in the wrong direction.*

He stares ferociously at the ball, then at SIEGFRIED. *The sky darkens and the rattle of machine guns is heard, along with the distant 'crump' of shellfire.* ANDERSON *raises his club in the air and, with a cry of attack, advances on* SIEGFRIED *as though to brain him.* SIEGFRIED, *who has sized up the situation, puts out his arms and holds him. The scene returns to normal as* ANDERSON *gradually recovers and adopts instant denial.*

I don't know what happened there. Did I slip in the mud?

SIEGFRIED. Nothing happened. We'll go to the clubhouse.

ANDERSON. If you insist. It *is* a bit warm.

(*As they go.*) We might even get ourselves a bite to eat. I'm feeling peckish, aren't you?

SIEGFRIED. Yes, just a little.

They have gone.

*

RIVERS*'s consulting room.* RIVERS *and* BILLY *are there.* RIVERS *is looking through* BILLY*'s file. After a few moments:*

BILLY. Aren't you going to say anything?

RIVERS *doesn't look up.*

RIVERS. I imagine the CO has already dealt with the matter.

BILLY. Yes, he's confined me to the hospital for a fortnight. Don't you think that's rather *extreme*?

RIVERS. It wasn't just a matter of being late back from town, though, was it? Sister Rogers says she saw you there without your armband on.

BILLY. I was looking for a girl. Which is not made easier by going around with a ribbon around your arm that practically announces 'I AM A LOONY'.

RIVERS. I gather you also made some crass remarks about Sister Rogers to the CO. Everything from her sexual orientation to the size of her feet. What do you *think* is going to happen if you carry on like that?

Tense, sullen pause. Then:

BILLY. Aren't you going to ask me if I found one?

RIVERS. One what?

BILLY. A girl?

RIVERS. No, I'm not.

BILLY. Her name is Sarah, and she's yellow all over. Don't you even want to know if I had it away with her?

RIVERS. No, I don't.

BILLY. You amaze me. All those questions of yours, and then when something interesting comes up, you don't want to know.

RIVERS *closes the file and pushes it away.*

RIVERS. You're right, I don't. What I *do* want to know is the cause of your loss of memory and why you're periodically unable to speak.

BILLY. Well, your wanting to know isn't helping. This isn't the treatment that I want.

RIVERS *is genuinely taken aback.*

RIVERS. What treatment *do* you want?

BILLY. Hypnosis.

RIVERS. *Hypnosis?* What put that into your mind?

BILLY. In the place that I was before, there was a Dr Sanderson who wanted to try it on me. Look it up in my file if you don't believe me.

RIVERS. I believe you. But I'm surprised you want it. People are often nervous about being hypnotised. They worry they'll be putting themselves in somebody else's power.

BILLY. Will they?

RIVERS. No.

BILLY. Then what's stopping you trying it out on me? It *is* used to get people's memory back, isn't it?

RIVERS. Yes, when everything else has failed. But in your case, everything else hasn't even been tried. For example, if your regimental files don't arrive, I'll have to write to your CO and ask *him* what happened on April the 23rd. And if he doesn't reply, you'll just have to remember it for yourself.

BILLY. Except I can't.

RIVERS. I realise that.

He stands.

Thank you, Mr Prior. That will be all.

BILLY (*with irony*). Thank *you*.

He goes. RIVERS *thinks a moment. Turns on his voice-recording instrument.*

RIVERS. Prior says that he wants hypnosis.
Should I believe him?
Or is he merely putting off the dreaded moment of remembering?
How do I explain to him that horror is natural?
That trauma flourishes in the dark?
He struggles to forget his horrors.
All of them do.
It's the English habit of suppressing what is unbearable.
Only Sassoon is different.
He remembers his horrors.
He treasures them.
He runs them through his fingers like a miser.
If it were not for them, he would have nothing to write.

*

SIEGFRIED*'s room. Two beds: one for him and one for* CAMPBELL. *Evening.* SIEGFRIED, *in a purple dressing gown, is cleaning a golf club. There's a knock at the door.*

SIEGFRIED. Hello?

The door opens cautiously. WILFRED *is there.*

WILFRED. Lieutenant Sassoon?

SIEGFRIED. Yes?

WILFRED. I'm, I'm sorry to disturb you.

SIEGFRIED. That's all right. Come in.

WILFRED does.

WILFRED. I wondered, would you… would you sign your book for me, please?

(*It's a slim book of verse.*) *The Old Huntsman.*

SIEGFRIED. Yes, of course.

He takes it.

WILFRED. I've brought a pen.

He hands it to SIEGFRIED.

SIEGFRIED. What name shall I write?

WILFRED. Susan Owen. My mother.

SIEGFRIED *looks at a page.*

SIEGFRIED. Page forty-two. Are you quite sure that she wants to read that 'Bert's gone syphilitic'? I had trouble even getting the publishers to print that.

WILFRED. I don't think it will come as any surprise to her. I tell her everything in my letters. Don't you?

SIEGFRIED. I think I've shocked her quite enough without any more searing revelations.

WILFRED. She must be very upset about your being in hospital.

SIEGFRIED. Not at all. I think it's one of her few comforts.

WILFRED. Really?

SIEGFRIED. Yes, she'd far rather have a son who was here in Dottyville, than a son who was being called a pacifist. You know why I'm here, I suppose?

WILFRED. Yes, I read your Declaration.

SIEGFRIED. What did you think of it?

WILFRED. I agreed with every word.

SIEGFRIED. I'm glad that somebody did.

He hands the book back to WILFRED.

WILFRED. Thank you. Um…

He gets more books out of his bag.

…there should be five altogether.

SIEGFRIED. Five? Has the War Office put it on a recommended reading list?

WILFRED. That's not very likely, is it? No, they're for my family.

He hands SIEGFRIED *a book.*

SIEGFRIED. Who's this one for?

WILFRED. My brother Harold. He's a midshipman in the Royal Navy Reserve.

SIEGFRIED (*writing*). Harold Owen?

WILFRED. Yes.

SIEGFRIED *signs and they exchange books.*

SIEGFRIED. And this one?

WILFRED. Mary Owen. My sister. She's just turned twenty-two. And…

SIEGFRIED *signs and they exchange books.*

…this one's for my cousin. Leslie Gunston.

He looks over SIEGFRIED*'s shoulder to check his spelling.*

G–U… that's right.

SIEGFRIED. Where is he stationed?

WILFRED. He isn't stationed anywhere. He has a mitral murmur in his heart. Well, that's the story. I'm not very admiring of it. But we're still friends. We show each other our poems, in fact.

He glances at SIEGFRIED, *hoping for some acknowledgement of his poetry-writing, but it's not forthcoming.* SIEGFRIED *indicates the book that* WILFRED *is holding:*

SIEGFRIED. And the last one is for you?

WILFRED. Yes.

SIEGFRIED. Hand it over.

> WILFRED *does, and then stays looking over* SIEGFRIED*'s shoulder.*

Sit down.

> WILFRED *sits.*

I can't sign it until you tell me your name.

WILFRED. Oh, I'm sorry. It's Owen. Wilfred Owen.

> SIEGFRIED *signs.*

I've been wanting to meet you ever since I heard you were here. But I didn't have the nerve to just, just wander up to you and, you know, parley in a casual way. That's where your book came in. But it's true that I'm a great admirer of it. I like 'The Death-bed' best.

SIEGFRIED. I *was* quite pleased with it.

WILFRED. I like 'The Redeemer' too.

> SIEGFRIED *flips through the book, in the way that writers do.* WILFRED *recites:*

> 'He faced me, reeling in his weariness,
> Shouldering his load of planks, so hard to bear.
> I say that He was Christ, who wrought to bless…'

I've been wanting to write something like that for years.

SIEGFRIED. Don't you think the Christ reference is rather lazy-minded? Jesus didn't go around sticking bayonets into Germans' stomachs.

> *He hands the book back to* WILFRED.

Was that tactless of me? You're not a Christian, are you?

WILFRED. I was when I was younger, but I'm not any more. I don't know what I am. I know I wouldn't want a religion that couldn't face up to the facts.

SIEGFRIED. What facts?

WILFRED. Well, if you call yourself a Christian, you can't leave out the bits that bother you, can you? If I *were* a Christian, I'd have to be a pacifist as well.

SIEGFRIED. And you're *not* a pacifist?

WILFRED. No, I'm not. Are you?

SIEGFRIED. No, I'm a soldier.

WILFRED. It's funny. All the time in France, I never thought about things like that.

SIEGFRIED. No, one's usually too busy to bother with ethical questions.

WILFRED. Or psychological ones.

SIEGFRIED. Or mystical ones.

WILFRED. That isn't always the case, though, is it?

SIEGFRIED. No?

WILFRED. No, I don't think so. Sometimes when you're alone, in the trenches, at night, you get the sense of something quite ancient there. As though there had always been trenches there. One trench we held, it had skulls packed into the earth all up the side. Like mushrooms. And it was easier to believe they were men from the Duke of Marlborough's army in seventeen-something, than to accept that they'd all been alive in the last two years. It's as if all other wars had somehow... distilled themselves into this war, and that made it into something you... almost couldn't challenge. Like a deep and powerful voice saying, 'Run along, little man. Be thankful if you survive.'

Embarrassed, he feels that it's time to go. He takes up the books.

Thank you for these. Oh, that reminds me. I'm editor of the hospital magazine. It's called *The Hydra*. I was wondering if you could let us have a poem to include in it?

SIEGFRIED. I probably can. I'll look for something.

WILFRED. Thank you. We'll appreciate it no end.

He's about to go, but the conversation feels somehow unfinished.

SIEGFRIED. I was going up with the rations one night and I saw the artillery pieces against the skyline and the flares going up. Just like one sees them every night. Only it seemed to me that I was seeing it from the future. I realised that a hundred years from now, they'll still be ploughing up skulls, and I felt that I was in the future, looking back to the way we were that night. I think I saw our ghosts.

Pause.

Did you say that *you're* a writer?

WILFRED. I didn't exactly, but I do write.

SIEGFRIED. Poetry?

WILFRED. Yes. Nothing in print yet.

SIEGFRIED. You could always show me some of your stuff, if you really want to.

WILFRED *laughs, amused by* SIEGFRIED*'s manifest lack of enthusiasm.*

WILFRED. You don't have to torture yourself!

SIEGFRIED. No, I mean it!

WILFRED. They *are* quite short.

SIEGFRIED. Yes, the war doesn't lend itself to epics.

WILFRED. Oh, I don't write about the war.

SIEGFRIED. Why not?

WILFRED. I… I've always thought the poetry *I* can write, is… it's a presumptuous thing to say, but I like to aim at something beautiful. I think the war's too ugly to write about.

SIEGFRIED. Isn't that like having a religion that can't face up to the facts?

WILFRED *thinks, puzzled.*

WILFRED. Maybe.

SIEGFRIED. You could bring me a poem next time we meet.

WILFRED. Well, as a matter of fact, I've got one here.

SIEGFRIED. Let's see it.

WILFRED *produces a notebook. Opens it, passes it over.*

WILFRED. I know I said they were all short, but this one's quite long. I wrote it for Captain Brock as part of my therapy.

SIEGFRIED *looks at the title.*

SIEGFRIED (*reads*). 'Antaeus'.

WILFRED. Yes.

SIEGFRIED. Why that?

WILFRED. That's what therapeutic about it. Antaeus was a giant who challenged Hercules to a wrestling match. And Hercules couldn't beat him, until he remembered that Antaeus was the son of Gaia, the goddess of the earth. And every time that Antaeus *touched* the earth, even if only with a toe, his mother would give him his strength back. So Hercules lifted him up into the air in a great bear-hug, and that's how he beat him. Dr Brock says his patients are like Antaeus, because we've been… 'upgrounded', he calls it… by the war.

SIEGFRIED *puts the poem to one side. Looks at* WILFRED, *as though seeing him for the first time.*

SIEGFRIED. Do you ever feel like strangling Brock?

WILFRED. No, we get on very well.

SIEGFRIED. My doctor is Captain Rivers.

WILFRED. Yes, I know.

SIEGFRIED. He's going on three weeks' holiday in the morning.

WILFRED. Maybe he needs a rest.

SIEGFRIED. It makes me bloody angry. I feel betrayed. I'll just have to concentrate on how glad I'll be that he's gone. He keeps reminding me that, after the war, people are going to ask me what I did. And that I'll have to reply, 'I spent three very comfortable years in a loony bin playing golf, while most of my friends got blown to smithereens.' He knows that I'll feel a total shit.

WILFRED *takes his time thinking through the following:*

WILFRED. I think… it takes time to get back to the way you were. When you were fit and well. And *once* that happens, I think you'll probably know that it's time. It'll come to you out of a blue sky.

SIEGFRIED. What happened to you? Why are you here?

WILFRED. I was blown sideways by a shell. There was no way of getting back to the line, so I hid in a railway cutting with a piece of corrugated iron over me. The officer I was with had caught it.

SIEGFRIED. Caught it how?

WILFRED *snaps.*

WILFRED. Do you really not know what that means? He was killed. Smashed to bits! I lay there smelling his stink for three days!

SIEGFRIED. I'm sorry.

WILFRED *passes it off.*

WILFRED. It was nothing. Only I started forgetting things all over the place. No use to anyone.

Pause.

I'm sorry I yelled. What'll you, what'll you do when this is all over?

SIEGFRIED. I've got no plans. What about you?

WILFRED. I'm going to keep pigs.

SIEGFRIED. *Pigs?*

WILFRED. Yes. People think pigs are dirty, but that's only if they're badly kept, and they're very intelligent. We had a piglet used to knock on the kitchen door to watch my brother and me having our tea.

SIEGFRIED. Are you a country man?

WILFRED. Through and through. From Shropshire. I'm mad about animals. I used to ride all day when I was a lad.

SIEGFRIED. There are horses here. We can ride together, if you like.

The door opens. It's CAMPBELL, *in pyjamas, slippers and dressing gown. He stares at* WILFRED *in surprise.*

CAMPBELL. I'm sorry, I seem to have the wrong room.

He twitches, then looks at the number on the door.

WILFRED. It's all right, Major Campbell. This *is* your room. I'm just leaving.

(*To* SIEGFRIED.) That poem for *The Hydra*. Don't forget.

SIEGFRIED. I won't. Goodnight.

WILFRED. Goodnight.

He goes. CAMPBELL *comes in, takes off his dressing gown, gets ready for bed.*

CAMPBELL. That's Owen, isn't it? Grammar-school type. (*Twitch.*) Not quite a sahib. (*Pronounced 'sarb'.*) By the way, you ought to know, they do a damn fine game of bridge in room number eighty-seven.

He twitches again.

Will you be wanting to read all night? Because I'm turning in post-haste, if it's all the same to you. (*Twitch.*)

SIEGFRIED (*quietly*). That's fine, go ahead.

He opens his book and reads. CAMPBELL *kneels by his bed and prays silently. Gets up and says to* SIEGFRIED, *amusedly abashed.*

CAMPBELL. One can't be too careful, can one?

He twitches and gets into bed. After some moments, a loud tapping noise is heard from nowhere in particular.

SIEGFRIED. What's that?

CAMPBELL. What's what?

SIEGFRIED. That tapping noise.

CAMPBELL. Sorry, old chap. Didn't hear a thing.

He taps one ear.

Shell-blast. I should imagine it was the wind.

He turns off the bedside light, if there is one, turns over and closes his eyes. SIEGFRIED looks at his book, but he can't concentrate. He hears the tapping again.

SIEGFRIED (*to* CAMPBELL). Don't tell me you can't hear that?

He falls silent, realising that CAMPBELL is asleep. Listens hard. The tapping is heard again. He gets up abruptly, opens the door, goes out of sight into the corridor.

(*Quietly.*) Hello? Is anyone there?

He comes back in, throws the door closed behind him and gets into bed…

… and we see, before he does, the ghost of a soldier, mud-spattered and bloody, revealed very suddenly by the closing of the door. This is EVANS. We hear the rumble of cannon and shellfire. EVANS looks at SIEGFRIED in a puzzled way. SIEGFRIED stares back. It is as though the two men know each other.

SIEGFRIED *leaps off his bed, runs out of the room…*

… and keeps on running. His route is long and indirect.

*

He arrives at RIVERS's consulting room, switching on the light as he enters.

The office is empty. SIEGFRIED stands in the middle of the room, puts his head in his hands. He cannot believe what's happened. He's terrified and in despair. He's still in his purple dressing gown, which now looks ridiculous.

SISTER ROGERS, *who is on night duty, comes in, having heard him running.*

SISTER ROGERS. Lieutenant Sassoon? What are you doing in here?

SIEGFRIED *stares at her, bewildered.*

SIEGFRIED. What?

SISTER ROGERS. I asked you why you are here? Do you know what time it is?

SIEGFRIED *struggles for words.*

SIEGFRIED. I'm... I'm...

Having got over her surprise, SISTER ROGERS *speaks gently and with compassion.*

SISTER ROGERS. There's no need to rush. Just take it gently.

With an effort, SIEGFRIED *pulls himself together.*

SIEGFRIED. What? You're Sister Rogers.

SISTER ROGERS. Yes.

SIEGFRIED. Where is he?

SISTER ROGERS. Do you mean Captain Rivers? Is it him that you're looking for?

SIEGFRIED. Yes.

SISTER ROGERS. He isn't here. He left on the overnight train. He'll be gone three weeks. He needs his rest, as I'm sure you know. He's quite worn out.

SIEGFRIED *nods.*

Go back to bed. I shall be on duty all night. You can ring the bell if you have any trouble.

She holds the door open.

Come on now.

SIEGFRIED. Thank you.

Still broken, he goes out. SISTER ROGERS *takes a quick glance around the office to see if anything is out of order and switches off the light.*

End of Act One.

ACT TWO

The sound of distant but enormous guns, as heard in London from the French battlefields.

*

RIVERS *waits in a corridor of the National Hospital, Queen Square, London. He has a cup of tea.* DR YEALLAND *appears.*

YEALLAND. Captain Rivers? I'm Dr Yealland. I hope I haven't kept you waiting?

RIVERS. No, not at all.

YEALLAND. Somebody's brought you a cup of tea, I see. That's more than they'll do for me these days. How are you finding London?

RIVERS. It's very different.

YEALLAND. Ah well, that's wartime for you. Sirens, Zeppelins.

RIVERS. Not to mention hearing the guns from France.

YEALLAND. Yes, one can almost imagine one is there.

RIVERS. I sometimes wish I were.

YEALLAND. Do you indeed? I think we're both too long in the tooth for that. War is a young man's game. You said in your letter that you would appreciate watching me apply the electric therapy.

RIVERS. If I could.

YEALLAND. Well, you're in luck, because the case that I have this morning ought to interest you no end. The man is mute. Dumb as an ox. I'm sure you've dealt with similar cases?

RIVERS. Yes, I had one very recently.

YEALLAND. My method of cure can be summed up in a single word. Can you guess what it is?

RIVERS. No, tell me.

YEALLAND. Chastisement. That is the key. Entirely effective and remarkably fast. I've seen men in the most appalling states and had them back at the front within a week. Not all of them fakers, either. All weaklings and degenerates though. Oh, yes, no doubt about it. Even if they'd stayed in civilian life, they would have had their little breakdowns sooner or later.

RIVERS. Do your patients ever relapse?

YEALLAND. Couldn't tell you. No idea.

RIVERS. Is there any incidence of suicide after the treatment?

YEALLAND. I shouldn't think so. Haven't heard of any.

They walk. YEALLAND *adds:*

As I say, you're welcome to watch, but I normally do these treatments on my own.

RIVERS. I'll be as unobtrusive as I can.

YEALLAND. Please do. The last thing these people need is a sympathetic audience.

*

They enter the electricity room. Electrical apparatus is visible. A terrified soldier named CALLAN *is seated in a chair.*

YEALLAND (*of him, to* RIVERS). This is Callan. Mons, the Marne, Aisne, first and second Ypres, Hill 60. Neuve-Chapelle, Loos. Armentières, the Somme and Arras.

RIVERS. A remarkable record.

YEALLAND *frowns.*

YEALLAND. Ssh.

(*To* CALLAN.) Have I missed out anywhere?

CALLAN *looks at him without expression.*

(*Quietly to* RIVERS.) Very negative attitude. He was employed behind the lines on transport, then last April, while feeding the horses, he fell to the ground, remained unconscious for five hours, and since then he hasn't uttered a word. Not one! Every treatment has been a failure.

RIVERS. What treatments has he had?

YEALLAND. Nothing out of the ordinary. Hot plates, lighted cigarettes to the tongue.

RIVERS *takes a seat on a chair in a corner.* YEALLAND *addresses* CALLAN, *very distinctly:*

Now I shall lock the door.

He does so, ostentatiously brandishing the key in CALLAN*'s direction before dropping it into his top pocket. He then prepares a pair of electrodes which are attached to a battery. Very clearly, as though to someone mentally challenged:*

Callan, I have seen many patients with conditions like yours, and they come into two categories, those who want to recover and those who do not. It makes no difference to me which group you belong to. All that matters is that you recover your speech. You will not leave this room until you have done so. Not one second earlier.

He depresses CALLAN*'s tongue with a spatula, applies an electrode to the back of his throat and turns a switch. Gagging,* CALLAN *is thrown back forcibly against the chair.*

No flinching, please. You must behave as the hero that your country believes you to be. A man who has been through so many battles should have better control of himself.

He fastens the straps around CALLAN*'s wrists.*

Remember you have to talk.

CALLAN *is white and shaking, but makes no sound.*

Nod when you are ready to speak.

No response.

Very well.

He reapplies the electrode. This time, CALLAN *convulses while emitting an almost-silent 'ah'.*

Did you hear that, Callan? Do you realise that a result has been achieved? Small as it may seem to you, if you will consider rationally for yourself, you will believe me when I tell you that it proves that you'll be talking before long.

He reapplies the electrode. CALLAN *convulses as before but this time, if he makes any sound at all, it is almost inaudible.*

Enough of that! Enough! Let us move on.

He unstraps CALLAN*'s wrists and helps him out of the chair.*

Walk up and down. Begin!

CALLAN *does as he is told, but very feebly.* YEALLAND *walks alongside him, supporting when he stumbles and reciting the letters of the alphabet for* CALLAN *to repeat.*

A. B. C. No, *A*. Try it again. *A*.

CALLAN, *who has managed only a series of faint 'ah's, suddenly breaks free, makes a dash for the door and attempts to wrest it open. Frustrated, he turns to* YEALLAND.

Callan, that was absurd of you. The door is locked and the key is in my hand.

He holds it up.

You will leave when you are cured, and not before. I have no doubt that you are tired and discouraged, but that is not my fault. The reason is purely that you do not understand your condition as well I do. Do you understand me?

Seemingly admitting defeat, CALLAN *points to the battery, miming 'Get on with it.'*

No, no, no. Suggestions are not wanted from you. They are beside the point. When the time comes to stimulate your throat once more, it will be done to you whether you want it or not.

(*With emphasis*.) You must speak, but the content does not interest me. I shall not listen to anything you say.

He leads CALLAN *back to the chair and straps him in.*

You are now ready for the next stage of treatment, which consists of the administration of strong shocks to the *outside* of the neck. You will soon be able to whisper anything you like.

He applies the electrode in the region of CALLAN*'s larynx, in short bursts. Each time,* CALLAN *responds with alphabetical 'ah', 'bah', 'cah', 'dah' sounds. Then, without any apparent cause, he gets stuck on 'bah', which he repeats, emitting a mocking sheep-like noise. But* YEALLAND *is gratified. He stands back.*

Are you not glad you have made such progress?

CALLAN *weeps, sobbing uncontrollably. After a moment:*

You must continue making sounds of some description. I do not care what the nature of a sound is. I shall *shape* it into *vowels*, and then *words* and finally *sentences*. Now utter a sound as soon as I touch your throat.

He applies the electrode to the larynx as before. CALLAN *doesn't respond, perhaps because his crying has only half-subsided. Suddenly and without warning,* YEALLAND*'s clinical detachment is replaced by naked anger. He grabs* CALLAN*'s wrists and looks him in the eye.*

This has gone on long enough. I may have to use a very much stronger current. I do not want to hurt you, but I will if I must.

He applies a stronger current to CALLAN*'s neck.* CALLAN *responds with an 'ah!' of pain and then with other, indeterminate, sounds.* YEALLAND *stands back.*

Better. Better. Tell me the days of the week.

CALLAN *utters an indeterminate shout.*

Try harder!

He gives CALLAN *another shock and* CALLAN *responds with a just-recognisable 'Sunday'.*

I said *days,* not *day!* All seven of them!

Slowly, CALLAN *answers him, his diction and voice a little clearer each time, though still very indistinct and foggy.*

CALLAN. Sunday.
  Monday.
  Tuesday.
  Wednesday.
  Thursday.
  Friday.
  Saturday.

YEALLAND. That is precisely what I required of you. Are you not pleased to be cured?

CALLAN *stands and smiles.*

I do not like your smile. I find it most objectionable. Sit down.

CALLAN *sits.* YEALLAND *applies an electrode to his mouth.* CALLAN *gasps and winces.*

Stand.

CALLAN *does.*

(*Very distinctly.*) Are You Not Pleased To Be Cured?

CALLAN *does not smile.*

CALLAN. Yes, sir.

YEALLAND. Nothing else?

CALLAN. Thank you, sir.

YEALLAND. That's better.

With some ceremony, he unlocks the door and opens it.

You may go.

He shows CALLAN *out of the room. Then glances at* RIVERS, *who fears that he's going to be sick.*

Captain Rivers, are you all right?

RIVERS. Could you direct me to the bathroom?

*

The grounds of Craiglockhart. Autumn. SIEGFRIED *and* WILFRED *are lounging or lying in what's left of the sunlight.* SIEGFRIED *is reading* The Loom of Youth *by Alec Waugh.* WILFRED *is reading* The Ballad of Reading Gaol. *After a few moments:*

WILFRED. Do you still have nightmares?

SIEGFRIED. Sometimes.

WILFRED. Bad ones?

SIEGFRIED. Very.

WILFRED. Have they got worse since Captain Rivers went away?

SIEGFRIED. That may be the timing, but it doesn't mean that's the reason. What about yours?

WILFRED. I've had a couple of bad nights. No more than that. Are you still missing Rivers?

SIEGFRIED. I miss having someone to talk to.

WILFRED. You can talk to me.

SIEGFRIED. I do, and I enjoy it when I'm in the mood, but you're not the same as him.

WILFRED. Is he your father-figure?

SIEGFRIED. I thought you wanted to read?

WILFRED. I will in a moment. Is that why you got so upset when he went on holiday? I'm thinking of your father leaving the family when you were five years old.

SIEGFRIED. What the devil makes you think there's any connection?

WILFRED. It came into my mind while I was shaving.

SIEGFRIED. Well, put it *out* of your mind. I don't go in for father-figures.

WILFRED. What about mother-figures?

SIEGFRIED. I don't like my mother.

WILFRED. Then maybe a mother-figure's what you need. Somebody sympathetic and protective. Maybe *that's* what Rivers is to you. I sometimes think we officers are more like mothers than we are like fathers. We talk gently to the men. We calm their fears. We examine their filthy nails. We put powder on their crusty feet and crystal violet on their gums.

SIEGFRIED. Stop prattling.

WILFRED. What I think that Rivers would say to you… if he were here… is that it's wrong for you to be stuck in Dottyville and it's time that you did something about it.

SIEGFRIED. What, for example?

WILFRED. You could tell him that you want to go to France, which I'm perfectly sure you do, and then he'll send a memorandum to the War Office and they'll have you there in a trice.

SIEGFRIED. Do you want me to go?

WILFRED. Don't be so stupid. I'd hardly be sitting here if I wanted you to go away. But I think you ought to.

SIEGFRIED. Out of duty?

WILFRED. I didn't say that.

SIEGFRIED. Because I love my country?

WILFRED. We all love our country. That's not the reason.

SIEGFRIED. Then why?

WILFRED. Because… it's very important that there's a poet in France. I mean… to honour the men who are doing the fighting. And to tell people at home what it's like for them. And, and it's… it's got to be you, because there isn't another poet who's as honest as you are.

He puts down his book.

(*With resolution.*) Speaking of which, have you read my poem?

SIEGFRIED. Mm-hm.

He takes out one of the notebooks in which WILFRED *writes and drafts his poems.*

WILFRED. All right, let's hear it. What do you think?

SIEGFRIED *looks at the poem.*

SIEGFRIED. It isn't bad. But it could be better.

WILFRED. I can make it better.

SIEGFRIED (*reads*). 'Anthem for Dead Youth'. Not a very good title.

WILFRED. It's the best I could think of. What else?

SIEGFRIED. You seem to have absorbed my style hook, line and sinker.

WILFRED. Is that bad?

SIEGFRIED. No, I don't think so.

WILFRED. Neither do I. Go on.

SIEGFRIED (*reading*).
    'What minute-bells for these who die so fast?
    Only the monstrous anger...'

WILFRED. Or it could be 'solemn' anger.

SIEGFRIED. Could it? Yes, maybe it could. What's a minute-bell?

WILFRED. It's a bell that warns people about a funeral. 'Passing bells' might be better.

SIEGFRIED. But if you lose 'minute', then you realise how weak 'fast' is.

He makes the change. Reads:

    'What passing-bells for those who die... so *fast*?'

WILFRED. You're right, it's feeble. What about... what about 'in herds'?

SIEGFRIED. Much better.

He makes the change.

The next line is very good.

WILFRED. It should be, after all the time I spent on it.

SIEGFRIED. I've no idea what you mean by 'all the time'. How long do you spend on a poem?

WILFRED. Fifteen minutes.

SIEGFRIED. That's not *nearly* enough!

WILFRED. I mean *every day*.

SIEGFRIED *laughs*.

SIEGFRIED. Listen to me. If you want to write anything remotely decent, you've got to sweat your guts out.

He hands WILFRED *the poem.*

Take this back and question every word and comma, over and over, as though it meant life and death. Then bring it to me, and I'll tell you what's wrong with it.

WILFRED *puts it away, half-crushed and half-flattered. A hat is thrown into view and a voice is heard calling:*

VOICE. Sassoon! Over here!

SIEGFRIED *kicks the hat back where it came from. Whoops and cheers are heard and a patient in uniform runs on with the hat. Another soldier tackles him, the hat is passed to another and…*

… swiftly the stage becomes the site of an informal match involving as many of the cast as can be spared, including WILFRED *and* SIEGFRIED, *though not* BILLY *or* RIVERS. *The game is hard and fast and joyous and covers the whole of the stage. This isn't a literal moment and it isn't in naturalistic time: it's a celebration of the men's youth and energy as it was before and perhaps will be again.*

RIVERS *appears. The game stops. He looks round at the men and smiles: he's glad to be back.*

RIVERS. Carry on.

The game resumes and travels out of sight. RIVERS *walks in the other direction, joining* SISTER ROGERS *en route. As a sickbay bed appears:*

SISTER ROGERS. It's a great pity that you were away while we had the inspection. We had no warning at all. The staff are very upset.

RIVERS. I'll talk to them.

SISTER ROGERS. Yes, do what you can. I fear the report on us might be discouraging. What other news. Lieutenant Copper has had a relapse. And Prior is in the sickbay again. He had a day at the seaside with the young lady he's been seeing...

RIVERS. Nothing wrong with that.

SISTER ROGERS. ...no, certainly not, but the train carriage on the way back was full of tobacco smoke, and he had another asthma attack. Fortunately the young lady managed to get him back here. She's just an ordinary working girl, but she seemed very sensible.

*

The sickbay. RIVERS *no longer has his overcoat and luggage: time has passed.* BILLY *is in an iron-framed bed, as when we saw him first. There's a chair by the side of the bed.*

RIVERS. I can't imagine how anyone thought it was a good idea to send an asthmatic to France. Or how you survived when you got there. Did you do the gas exercises?

BILLY. Everyone does.

RIVERS. Did they send you through the huts?

BILLY. No, they didn't try that. I wouldn't have lasted a minute in there. But my minimal lung capacity has its uses.

RIVERS. What are they?

BILLY. I'm the first to know when the German gas is coming. I'm the miners' canary.

RIVERS. On the other hand, if you collapsed in battle and somebody carried you, you'd slow him down and you'd probably both get killed.

BILLY. Now you've really cheered me up. If I get any worse, will I get sent to another hospital?

RIVERS. Don't you want that?

BILLY. No, I don't.

RIVERS. I thought you didn't like it here.

BILLY. You can get used to anything, can't you?

RIVERS. Should I take that as a compliment?

BILLY. Yes, if you like. Look what I dug out from the hospital library. (*Produces a book from the side of his bed and hands it to* RIVERS.) *Sex and Society in the Solomon Islands.*

RIVERS. I didn't know you were interested in anthropology.

BILLY. I am now. How long did it take you to write?

RIVERS. About six months.

BILLY. Their sex lives are impressive. Do they really carry on like that?

RIVERS. They certainly do.

BILLY. They must be knackered. I wouldn't be able to keep it up. Could you keep it up, Dr Rivers?

Like all doctors, RIVERS *is used to patients flirting with him, but he hadn't expected* BILLY *to do so. He replies soberly:*

RIVERS. I think my age and your asthma might present us from setting any records.

BILLY. You do a wonderful imitation of a stuffed shirt. And you're not like that at all, really, are you? Haven't you got a secret life hidden away somewhere?

RIVERS (*a reminder to get on with it*). Mr Prior.

BILLY. Sorry.

He puts down the book.

How can I help you, *Dr* Rivers?

RIVERS. Before I went away, we talked about a possible link between your mutism and your memory-loss.

BILLY. I don't want to talk about that.

RIVERS *decides to humour him.*

RIVERS. What *do* you want to talk about?

BILLY. Something you said last time I saw you. You said that officers don't suffer from mutism.

RIVERS. It's rare.

BILLY. How many cases have you got?

RIVERS. There was you and one other, and now there aren't any. In my previous post, where I was treating private soldiers, it was the commonest symptom by a long way.

BILLY. Why?

RIVERS. Well… I imagine that mutism springs from a, a conflict between *wanting* to say something, and knowing that if you *do* say it, it will work out badly for you. And it'll be worse for a private soldier than it would for an officer. So the private becomes unable to speak at all. Whereas officers do the same thing halfway. They stammer. There are other differences as well. Officers' dreams are more elaborate than the men's, I suppose because the officers have a more complex mental life.

BILLY *reacts as though he's been stung.*

BILLY. Are you serious? You honestly believe that that *gaggle* of noodle-brained halfwits has a *complex mental life*?

RIVERS. Yes, most of the time, because officers have a longer education.

BILLY. How do I fit into that? 'Cause I've got practically *no* education.

RIVERS. Well, it's interesting that you don't stammer.

BILLY. It's even more interesting that you *do*.

RIVERS *is taken aback.*

RIVERS. That's d… different.

BILLY. How is it different?

RIVERS. In the case of, of a lifelong stammerer like myself… from earliest childhood… I don't think anyone knows the cause. It could even be genetic.

BILLY*'s tone becomes first sharp, then hostile.*

BILLY. That's lucky for you, isn't it? Because if your stammer was the same as your patients have got, you might have to sit down and work out what it *is* that you've spent your entire life trying *not* to say.

RIVERS. Is that the end of my appointment?

BILLY *turns over and disappears under a sheet.*

You know, one day you're going to have to accept the fact that you're in this hospital because you're ill. Not me. Not Sister Rogers. Not the kitchen porter. *You.*

BILLY *pulls the sheet more firmly over his head.* RIVERS *goes.*

*

The clubhouse at the golf links. ROBERT GRAVES *is at a table with a book.* SIEGFRIED *appears fresh from a round of golf.*

SIEGFRIED. Sorry I'm late.

GRAVES. Don't worry about it. Your friend Owen was keeping me amused. But then he had to go into town to see a printer.

SIEGFRIED. He edits the hospital magazine.

GRAVES. He told me that. We had a good old chat about those poems of his you sent me.

SIEGFRIED. I hope you didn't discourage him. His stuff is very unequal, but I do think some of it shows promise.

GRAVES. 'Promise'? '*Promise*'? Sass, are you out of your mind? That boy is the real thing.

SIEGFRIED. Do you think so?

GRAVES. Bloody know it! No mistake! Excellent poet, that fellow.

SIEGFRIED *is surprised in a not altogether pleasant way.*

SIEGFRIED. I'm delighted you think so.

GRAVES. The only *slightly* critical thought I had... which I went so far as to tell him, in a tactful way of course... was that, now, how can I put it...?

SIEGFRIED. They're a bit rough?

GRAVES. No, I like the roughness. It goes with the energy. No, I was going to say that one or two of the poems are a bit Sassoonish.

SIEGFRIED. *What?*

Impervious, GRAVES *continues:*

GRAVES. But he's got some fine stuff in there. I was especially taken by the half-rhymes... 'burn, born'... 'brambles, rumbles'...

SIEGFRIED. To be entirely fair, I don't think Owen is the first poet in the world to have invented para-rhyme.

GRAVES. No, *I* invented para-rhyme.

He quotes from memory:

> 'Must we henceforth be *grateful*
> That the guards, though *spiteful*...'

...and so on and so on. But it's a credit to Owen, how well he does it. And all credit to you for finding him.

SIEGFRIED *is doing his best not to show how bruising he finds this conversation.*

SIEGFRIED. *He* found *me*, in fact. Let's not talk about poetry over lunch. It isn't civilised.

Annoyed, he arranges his golf bag.

GRAVES. Decent game?

SIEGFRIED. Not bad.

GRAVES. You said in a letter that you were attacked by a lunatic on the links.

SIEGFRIED. That was weeks ago. He was in a filthy mood because his wife hadn't turned up. In fact she never turns up. I think she may be a figment of his imagination.

A WAITER *is there.*

Did you have time to look at the menu?

GRAVES. I had time to memorise it.

(*To the* WAITER.) The shepherd's pie, and a pint of draught.

SIEGFRIED. Ditto.

The WAITER *goes.*

GRAVES. You must be going up before the board before very long?

SIEGFRIED. End of the month.

GRAVES. I'd say that, from the narrative point of view, that's pretty good timing.

SIEGFRIED. What are you talking about?

GRAVES. Well, you're a writer, old chap. Just think how the story goes. Opening chapter: war hero goes off his head, pens a peculiar Declaration, talks gobbledegook, becomes the despair of all his friends.

SIEGFRIED. Are you being serious?

GRAVES. Chapter two: he spends three months out of the public eye, arduous treatment, genius doctor. Are you with me?

SIEGFRIED. Carry on.

GRAVES. Final chapter: recuperation! His sanity is restored, he makes a shining appearance in front of the medical board and goes back to the front without a *shadow* over his reputation. What do you say?

SIEGFRIED. What I did was…

He stops for a moment.

…it was nothing to do with fiction. It wasn't a *story*. It was real. I meant every word. Profoundly. Deeply. I was appalled by the war and I still am. I cannot believe that all sides can't sit down and forge some kind of a peace. To hell with our pride. To hell with our dignity. One hundred and two thousand men were killed last month *alone*. I can't acquiesce

in that, and neither should you. Nor *would* you, if you had
any moral courage.

GRAVES (*stiff*). I have a smatter of courage, I believe. But I
prefer to keep my word.

SIEGFRIED. So do I. But I didn't put on my uniform in order
to…

GRAVES *tops him.*

GRAVES. When you put on your uniform, you signed a
contract, Sass. And you can't back out of it merely because
you've changed your mind. You have to buckle down and do
the job that you promised to do. Just like the hundreds of
thousands of poor blighters out there…

He gestures as if towards France.

…who're being shelled and blinded and drowned in the mud.
Not one in a *thousand* of whom has had your privileges in
life. Do you think you can turn round to them and say that
you've changed your mind about the war? Do you know
what their answer will be? They'll say you're not behaving
like a gentleman, and that's the most damning thing they can
say about anybody.

He stares at SIEGFRIED.

Do you hear me?

SIEGFRIED. I refuse to listen.

He stands up and goes.

*

RIVERS*'s consulting room. Evening.* RIVERS *speaks into
his recording device.*

RIVERS. Yealland's method of treatment was as disgusting as I
had feared.
Thank God our methods aren't the same.
But are our aims any different?
We both coerce young men back to the slaughterhouse.

There is a knock at the door. RIVERS *calls:*

One moment!

He dictates:

One could coerce Sassoon very easily.
Courage is in his nature.
It's his determining characteristic.
But I have too much respect for him to try.
And thanks to him…

He thinks for a moment.

Thanks to him, I have too little respect for the war.

He turns off the recording device and calls:

Come in.

The door opens. It's BILLY, *fully dressed.*

BILLY. I came to say that I'm sorry about this morning.

RIVERS. You needn't apologise. If you'd *really* wanted to be offensive, you could have done a lot better.

BILLY. I did consider asking you if you'd fucked any of your Solomon Islanders.

RIVERS. What stopped you?

BILLY. I thought it wasn't any of my business.

RIVERS. You're right, it isn't.

BILLY. Besides, there's not much point in offending you, if all I get back is a wave of weary tolerance.

RIVERS. You don't *want* to offend me. You keep *behaving* as though you'd just said something incredibly shocking but you've never actually done so. Except a moment ago, and that was just showing off.

A short silence. BILLY *sits, although* RIVERS *hasn't invited him to.*

BILLY. I wish I hadn't got ill. I want to go into town.

RIVERS. To see your girl?

BILLY. That too. Also the nightmares are worse when I'm stuck indoors.

RIVERS. Do you want to talk about them now?

BILLY. Look, they're just…

He laughs.

…'*Standard issue battle nightmares. Potty officers for the use of.*'

His tone changes, becomes more serious.

Except that sometimes they get muddled up with sex. And when I wake up…

He stops, glances evasively at RIVERS, *then at his crotch.*

…I find I've spouted. It makes me lose all self-respect. I've even wondered if there's any point in going on.

RIVERS *mentally runs through the several things he could say, before settling on one.*

RIVERS. We could try hypnosis, if you liked.

BILLY. Now?

RIVERS. Yes, why not? It's the time of day we're least likely to be interrupted.

BILLY. Will it get me well enough to go back to France?

RIVERS. I can't promise you that. But it might drive those hateful thoughts out of your mind.

BILLY. It's funny. When you said a lot of people were frightened of hypnosis, I didn't believe you. But now I'm frightened.

RIVERS. We can leave it till later.

BILLY. No, I can't pester you and then turn it down.

He braces himself.

What do I do?

RIVERS. It's very simple.

He turns out a light or two, leaving the room more dimly lit.

Relax. Sit back in the chair.

BILLY *does.*

You're tensing up.

RIVERS *lightly touches his shoulders.*

Shoulders.

BILLY *relaxes.*

Now your hands. Let the wrists go.

BILLY *relaxes further.*

Comfortable?

BILLY *nods.* RIVERS *picks up a pen.*

I want you to look at this pen. Don't raise your head. Just your eyes.

BILLY *looks.*

That's right. I'm going to count down from ten. By the time I get to zero, you'll be in a light sleep. All right?

BILLY *nods.*

Ten… Nine… Eight… Seven… Your eyelids are heavy now. Don't fight it, let them close. Six… Five… Four… Three… Two…

He waits a while. BILLY *is still.*

Tell me what you see. No need to hurry. Let it come.

Lights dim, except on BILLY.

BILLY. Sandbags. Smell of the wet. Smell of people. There's a candle on table, stuck down in its own wax. Bottles, mugs, the field telephone. It's nearly sparrow-fart. Be set to go in a minute. There's Mellors yelling out 'Stand-to!' We climb up out of the dugout, but it's a muddy slide, keep slithering back. Hello there! Somebody's fryin' bacon. (*Grins.*) It's Sawdon and Towers making tea on a tiny fire. Towers is singing quietly to hisself. Daft song of 'is.

He quietly sings a popular parody of 'After the Ball was Over', remembering:

'After the ball was over,
See her take out her glass eye.
Hang her cork leg on the bedpost,
Shake out a bottle of dye…'

He laughs.

'Come on, you gutsy bugger,' I say, 'Gissa a cup.' He hands
it over. 'Anything for you, sir.' Tin mug. Tastes of chemicals.
Walk on for a bit. Clear blue sky. Dozy morning. Fuck,
spoke too soon.

*There's the noise of a shell howling through the air and
landing.*

Whoop of a shell. Where's it landed?

He turns to see.

Brown smoke billowing up where I just come from. Nearly
break my neck running back. Bloody great hole. Fire gone,
tea gone, bacon gone. Towers and Sawdon gone as well.
Both blown to buggery.

*He pants as though he's been running, sinks his head in his
hands. The noise of battle begins: machine guns, shouting
and cannon.*

Grab a shovel. Pile the bone and flesh and earth tits-up into a
sandbag. Here's Logan, he's helping me clear up the mess.
He's muttering, 'Fuck, fuck, fuck.' Passes his bottle of rum
and I help myself. Keeps down the sick. I look down to the
duckboards and I'm staring… yes, I'm staring right into an
eye. It's blue, bright blue. Pick it up with two fingers. Now
I'm holding it out to Logan like a sweetie. I ask him, 'What
do I with this gobstopper?' He looks at me oddly, takes it.
What's he saying to me? 'Me and Williams'll finish this up,
sir. You go back.' He's walking me down to the Casualty
Station. Now I'm there. My tongue and my throat are dumb.
Can't make a sound. Lad lying next to me keeps muttering,
'I'm cold, I'm cold.' I remember what happened before. I
can almost hear it. Two of my men were killed this morning.
It seems quite normal to me now. Being dumb seems normal
as well. I sit and wait. I think about nothing. Empty.

The sounds of battle fade and the scene returns to normal.
BILLY *opens his eyes. Stares at* RIVERS.

(*Angrily.*) *Is that all?*

RIVERS. Why 'all'? I would have thought it was traumatic, finding the, the...

BILLY. It wasn't the fucking *eyeball*. Don't you *understand*?

Puts his head in his hands, begins to cry. RIVERS *offers him his handkerchief but, instead of taking it,* BILLY *seizes him by the arms and butts him in the chest, over and over, like a billy goat. After a while he stops.*

There was a man I knew who took out a patrol. They came across what he thought was a German wiring party, so he ordered his men to open fire. But they were ours. British soldiers. Five of 'em killed, eleven injured. He'd done the worst thing that a man could do. And now with Sawdon and Towers gone... and I'm standing with their tin mug in my hand... I thought I'd done the same thing meself. I thought it was all my fault.

He cries.

RIVERS. But there's no connection. Your men didn't die because of you. You even cleaned the trench.

BILLY. I've cleaned dozens of trenches. Why would two blown-up soldiers drive me mad?

RIVERS. It's never just one event. It's weeks and months of stress. They wear you down.

BILLY. And what does that say about me? I cracked up.

RIVERS. Billy, it's absolutely normal for those who escape the killing to feel a burden of guilt. I do it myself.

BILLY. Do you *really*? Tell me the truth. Don't make it easy for me.

RIVERS. It's the truth.

BILLY. So if I'm just like other people... what's to stop the medical board passing me fit for action?

RIVERS. Other people don't have your asthma.

BILLY. Well, if you're thinking of using *that* to wangle me out of the fighting, you can save yourself the trouble, because I don't want it.

RIVERS. Why not?

BILLY. *Why not?* Because after the war, people who didn't go to France… or men who didn't do well when they were there… those sad buggers aren't going to count for a damn thing. Fighting a Good War in France will be the club to end all clubs.

RIVERS. And you want to be a member?

BILLY. Yes, I've *got* to be.

RIVERS. But you belong to that club already.

BILLY. No, I failed it. I broke down, and I got expelled.

RIVERS. Is that why you want to go back?

BILLY *nods.*

You're ambitious, aren't you? What do you want to do when the war's over?

BILLY. Politics.

RIVERS. Not a bad idea.

BILLY. Nah, it's useless. You can't get anywhere in this country without an Oxford or Cambridge degree.

RIVERS. That's rubbish, Billy. I didn't get a degree from either. Besides, things will be different then. Hundreds of thousands of young men will have fought side by side with the working classes. They'll want to see them getting a better deal.

BILLY. You sound like a Bolshevik.

RIVERS. I'm trying to give you faith in your own abilities. That's all.

BILLY *goes to the door. Stops, turns. It's as though a weight has been lifted from his shoulders.*

BILLY. It were Harry Towers' eye. His eyes were blue. We used to call him the Hun. Goodnight.

RIVERS. Sleep well.

BILLY *goes.*

*

The Conservative Club. SIEGFRIED *is waiting in an armchair, a gin and tonic by his side.* RIVERS *arrives.*

RIVERS. I'm sorry I kept you waiting. I had a long meeting.

SIEGFRIED. Don't worry about it. I amused myself in the library looking at the old codgers.

RIVERS *looks around.*

RIVERS. The ones on the wall, or the ones in the armchairs?

SIEGFRIED. Both, of course. But the armchair ones are the ones I hate. You should have seen the evil bastards, drooling in anticipation of the Next Big Push.

RIVERS. This *is* the Conservative Club.

SIEGFRIED. I'd not forgotten. Have you any particular reason for inviting me here?

RIVERS. I thought that it would be pleasant to meet more sociably than we normally do.

A Scottish WAITER *is there.*

WAITER. What can I get you, gentlemen?

RIVERS. Whisky and water for me. What're you drinking, Siegfried?

SIEGFRIED. Gin and tonic.

WAITER. They will be with you in one moment, sir.

The WAITER *goes.*

SIEGFRIED. How was your holiday?

RIVERS. It was fine up to a point, and then I had an experience so appalling that it made me question everything I've done since the war began.

SIEGFRIED. What was it?

RIVERS. You're not supposed to ask questions. That's what *I* do!

He laughs.

I've had some very depressing news. Craiglockhart has fallen out of favour with the War Office. They think an excess of experimental thinking has turned it into a playpen for dodgers and degenerates. The CO is getting the sack.

SIEGFRIED. Will you replace him?

RIVERS. No, I can't do the dirty on him. Besides, I've been offered another job. Psychologist with the Royal Flying Corps.

SIEGFRIED. Will you take it?

RIVERS. Oh, I think so. It won't affect too many of my patients. Anderson will be discharged after the next board. Owen as well.

SIEGFRIED. Where will Owen be sent?

RIVERS. General duties somewhere. He'll be very upset, I imagine.

SIEGFRIED. I suppose he will. Who else is leaving?

RIVERS. What about you?

SIEGFRIED. Why me?

RIVERS. That's for you to decide. I'm not going to press you one way or the other. But I think you know what you *ought* to do.

SIEGFRIED. You want me to go back on everything that I wrote in my Declaration?

RIVERS. Not at all. You don't have to pretend that the war is being fought for sensible reasons, or that it isn't being run by numbskulls.

(*With emphasis.*) Just be *true to your nature*.

SIEGFRIED. What do you know about my nature?

RIVERS. I know what you've told me. So I consider I know it well. The question is, do *you*?

The WAITER *arrives with their drinks. Each takes a sip.*

SIEGFRIED. While you were away... I saw something that I couldn't have seen.

RIVERS. You mean another hallucination?

SIEGFRIED. Either that or a ghost.

RIVERS. Go on.

SIEGFRIED. It began with a tapping noise. I went into the corridor, but there was nobody there so I went back into my room. And a man was standing inside the door. A man I knew quite well. Lieutenant Evans. Nice lad. He was killed six months ago.

RIVERS. Was he like the figures that you saw in London?

SIEGFRIED. Not at all. There, they were clutching the holes in their heads and waving their stumps about. It seems you get a better class of ghost in Scotland. I don't expect a man of science like you to believe me.

RIVERS. I believe you *saw* him. I heard a ghost once, in the Solomon Islands. One of the islanders had died in a fire with the rest of his family. The people there believe that the spirits will arrive in a canoe to take away the souls of the dead, so… that particular night, the entire village was waiting in this big communal house. And at about midnight, they started saying that they could hear the paddles approaching. I didn't hear anything myself. But then a few moments later, when the spirits were supposedly inside the room, the entire house started to reverberate with whistling sounds. Extremely loud. No one was making them, but everyone heard them.

SIEGFRIED. Were you frightened?

RIVERS. No, I was very moved. You see, I'd very much liked the man who died. How did you feel about yours?

SIEGFRIED. I felt guilty.

RIVERS. Did you think he was angry with you?

SIEGFRIED. No, he was puzzled. He couldn't understand what I was doing in a hospital in Scotland. The next morning I wrote a poem about him.

He quotes from memory:

'And while the dawn begins with slashing rain
I think of the Battalion in the mud.
"When are you going back to them again?
Are they not still your brothers through our blood?"'

RIVERS. Does that question have an answer?

Pause.

SIEGFRIED. Yes. I'm going back to France.

RIVERS. When did you decide?

SIEGFRIED. Right now. This minute. I'll want a written guarantee from the War Office that I'll be posted to active service. I've no intention of shuffling files for the rest of the war.

RIVERS. What makes you think you can pick and choose?

SIEGFRIED. Because you'll speak up for me. I want you to promise the board that I'm fit to fight. Because it's true and you know it is. There's nothing wrong with me now and there never has been. Will you do that?

The WAITER *is there.*

WAITER (*to* RIVERS). Your table is ready, sir.

RIVERS (*to* SIEGFRIED). Shall we go through?

They leave. As they do so…

…rumble of shellfire.

*

The shellfire continues as the medical board appears with a sense of ominousness and pomp. The members take their places facing upstage. RIVERS *takes his place at one end of the line.* BILLY *faces the board. He's very nervous.*

MEDICAL OFFICER TWO. Would you say, Mr…

MEDICAL OFFICER THREE. Prior.

MEDICAL OFFICER TWO.…would you say that your memory has returned *in toto*?

BILLY. Returned in what, sir?

MEDICAL OFFICER ONE. Your *memory*, Prior.

MEDICAL OFFICER THREE (*standing for no nonsense*). Aren't we making too much of this? His memory isn't *essential*, is it? As long as he remembers where the enemy is?

MEDICAL OFFICER ONE. In which case he's fit for combat. Are there any comments?

RIVERS. There is another factor.

BILLY *looks suspiciously at* RIVERS.

MEDICAL OFFICER TWO. Is there?

MEDICAL OFFICER THREE. What?

RIVERS. Lieutenant Prior has had two asthma attacks since arriving at Craiglockhart, and they were both severe enough to confine him to bed. If he has an attack like that in battle, he'll be a danger both to himself and to others. You'll find a report among your papers.

The board members look at their papers.

MEDICAL OFFICER ONE. Ah.

Then:

Prior, you will recuse yourself.

BILLY. Do you mean I can go, sir?

MEDICAL OFFICER ONE. Yes, go!

(*As* BILLY *leaves.*) Permanent home service, I would say. Are we all agreed?

They are.

That's this afternoon's roster dealt with, with the exception of Lieutenant Sassoon. But I don't propose that we wait for him.

MEDICAL OFFICER TWO. Damned impertinent of the fellow not to attend.

As the medical board dissolves, RIVERS *leaves and crosses paths with* SISTER ROGERS.

RIVERS. Sister Rogers, have you seen Sassoon?

SISTER ROGERS. I thought he was going before the board?

RIVERS. No, he didn't turn up!

SISTER ROGERS. Then he must be somewhere in the grounds. And may I suggest that you speak to Prior? He's very upset. I didn't know what to say to him for the best.

RIVERS *sees* SIEGFRIED.

RIVERS (*calling*). Sassoon!

SIEGFRIED *appears. He and* RIVERS *stand facing each other some distance apart. No one else is onstage.*

SIEGFRIED. Yes?

RIVERS. I suppose you have an explanation?

SIEGFRIED. I waited more than an hour. I thought that was long enough, so I left. It was discourteous of the board to keep me waiting.

RIVERS. What about the courtesy due to the board? Or the CO of this hospital? Or even *me*? Don't you think we're due some kind of explanation of your walking out?

SIEGFRIED. I couldn't face it.

RIVERS. So it was cowardice?

SIEGFRIED. No, it was petulance. I thought that if I was going to offer up my life, the least other people could do was be on time.

RIVERS. Are you saying you've changed your mind?

SIEGFRIED. No.

RIVERS. Then I struggle to make sense of what you're telling me. Are you going back to the war or are you not?

SIEGFRIED. I am.

RIVERS. Thank God for that.

He takes off his spectacles and polishes them with his handkerchief.

I've heard from London. They agree with me that you're fully recovered from the breakdown that you never had, so they won't stand in the way of your going to France.

SIEGFRIED. You seem angry.

RIVERS. I don't pretend to understand what you're really up to. You're the most baffling human being I've ever met.

He extends a hand and they shake hands.

Good day to you.

SIEGFRIED. And to you.

He goes. RIVERS *moves away and discovers* BILLY, *who is sitting somewhere, scrunched up with his arms around his knees, very upset.*

RIVERS. Billy?

BILLY *turns and looks at him.*

BILLY. 'Permanent home service.' That's what they've given me. And you *wangled* it! You pulled my *asthma* out of the bag to stop me going. What was *that* all about?

RIVERS. Billy, you hate me because I got you something that you're ashamed of wanting. But it's nothing to be ashamed of, is it? Wanting to stay alive?

BILLY. Wouldn't you be ashamed?

RIVERS. Yes, I probably would be, but I hope I'd have the sense to see how ridiculous I was being.

BILLY (*bitterly*). You don't understand. I've *never* allowed my asthma to hold me back. Even as a kid, I always beat the others. Running, jumping, climbing a wall. My mother shut me up in the house. To keep me away from the nasty, rough boys. And here you are doing the same.

RIVERS. Is that who you think I am? Your mother?

BILLY. What else should I think? You fuss after me like a lovely big fat clucking hen.

He looks at RIVERS, *almost with affection.*

Oh, I don't hate you. I'm grateful to you for putting up with me. I was a brat.

RIVERS. No, you weren't.

BILLY. Can I come and visit you after the war?

RIVERS. I'll be delighted if you do. The staff here will know where I've got to. If I don't see you till then, good luck to you, Billy.

BILLY. Good luck to you.

They part.

∗

The Conservative Club. The dining room: a well-laid table and sparkling cloth. WILFRED *and* SIEGFRIED *are seated.* WILFRED *looks around in mixed wonderment and derision.*

WILFRED. What made you pick the Conservative Club?

SIEGFRIED. Rivers brought me here for lunch the other day and it gave me a taste for the high life. The food is adequate, the wines are extraordinary and they even have bedrooms upstairs for old Scottish Tories who've drunk too much to stagger off home.

WILFRED. Does Rivers treat *all* his patients to lunch here? Or just the blue-blooded ones?

SIEGFRIED. Don't be chippy. And since you mention it, my blood is as lacking in blue as that of my forefather Moses.

WILFRED. What're you talking about? You're not Jewish.

SIEGFRIED. My ancestors were.

WILFRED. Is that why you're called Siegfried?

SIEGFRIED. No, the reason I'm called Siegfried is that my mother so adores the works of Wagner that she thinks the greatest disaster of the war is that she can't go to the Bayreuth Festival. If I'd been born a girl, she would have christened me Brünnhilde.

He sings 'Hojotoho! Hojotoho!' and brandishes a knife as though it were a Wagnerian spear.

WILFRED. Why are you being like this? All laughing and silly? It's our last evening, and I feel as if I've just met you.

SIEGFRIED. I'm getting carried away by sentiment.

WILFRED. By our saying 'goodbye', you mean?

SIEGFRIED. Well, not for ever. But I don't look forward to another four weeks at Craiglockhart without you there.

WILFRED. I won't be far, thanks to the medical board. Only in Scarborough washing dishes. You'll be in France long before I get there.

SIEGFRIED. If you go to France, I'll stick a knife in your leg. You're too valuable to lose.

The WAITER *wheels a trolley into sight and serves dinner. Wine is already on the table.* SIEGFRIED *pours, spilling a little. He mops it up, pours.*

How are you for time?

WILFRED. No hurry at all. Waverley Station, ten past midnight. And if I happen to miss the train, there'll be another at half-past six in the morning. I could even stay here for the night.

Embarrassed, he drinks.

SIEGFRIED. So what do you think?

WILFRED, *hearing this as an invitation, is almost too churned-up to speak.*

WILFRED. What do I think about what?

SIEGFRIED. The wine.

WILFRED. It's very good. Why don't you tell me about it later. Where it comes from, what it's made of. I've got something to show you.

He takes out his scrappy notebook and hands it to SIEGFRIED, *who looks at it.*

SIEGFRIED. What draft is this?

WILFRED. Lost count. You did tell me to sweat my guts out.

SIEGFRIED. I can't believe I used that vulgar phrase.

(*Reading*.) 'Anthem for Dead Youth'.

WILFRED. Let me.

He takes back the notebook and reads, looking across at
SIEGFRIED *from time to time to see his reaction.*

'What passing-bells for these who die as cattle?
Only the monstrous anger of the guns.
Only the stuttering rifles' rapid rattle
Can patter out their hasty orisons.
No mockeries now for them; no prayers nor bells,
Nor any voice of mourning save the choirs, –
The shrill, demented choirs of wailing shells;
And bugles calling to them from sad shires.

What candles may be held to speed them all?
Not in the hands of boys, but in their eyes
Shall shine the holy glimmers of good-byes.
The pallor of girls' brows shall be their pass;
Their flowers the tenderness of patient minds,
And each slow dusk a drawing-down of blinds.'

He looks over at SIEGFRIED, *questioning. For the first
time,* SIEGFRIED *feels the full force of the younger man
being the better poet.*

Well?

SIEGFRIED. It's… *tremendously* good. I'm very impressed.

WILFRED *nods palely, waiting for more.* SIEGFRIED
continues:

Though when you look at the *sense* of it… you've
contradicted yourself, haven't you? You start by saying
there's no consolation, and then you say there is. Listen:

'Not in the hands of boys, but in their eyes
Shall shine the holy glimmers of good-byes.'

WILFRED. That isn't consolation. It's pride in the sacrifice.
You did the same thing in 'Prelude'.

SIEGFRIED. Well… you know what you're doing. I think you
should publish it.

WILFRED. In *The Hydra*?

SIEGFRIED. No, in a proper weekly. Let me send it to the *Nation* for you. But it needs a different title. 'Anthem for…'

He crosses out a word, substitutes another.

'Anthem for *Doomed* Youth'.

He smiles at WILFRED.

I'm sure they'll print it.

WILFRED. Thank you.

SIEGFRIED. It was a pleasure. This is for you.

He gets out an envelope and passes it to WILFRED.

Don't open it now.

WILFRED. Why not?

SIEGFRIED. You can read it later.

WILFRED. No, I can't wait.

He opens it. Takes out a smaller envelope. There's a letter inside.

SIEGFRIED. It's a letter of introduction to Robert Ross. He's the friend of Oscar Wilde's I told you about. Half Moon Street, off Piccadilly. He has a set of stunningly beautiful rooms, all lined in dusty gold.

WILFRED *looks at the letter, then finds something else.*

WILFRED. What's this doing here?

He takes out a banknote.

SIEGFRIED. It's from me. I want you to enjoy your leave.

He realises from WILFRED'*s silence that something has gone wrong.*

What is it?

WILFRED. A ten-pound note?

SIEGFRIED. Yes?

WILFRED. I can't believe it. We're saying goodbye... for who knows how long... and you behave as though I was a little schoolboy and you were my rich uncle. Is that what you think of me?

SIEGFRIED. I didn't mean to embarrass you.

WILFRED *is incredibly upset, close to tears.*

WILFRED. It's *worse* than embarrassing. That doesn't come close, you know? It breaks my heart. I thought this might be a letter from you. I thought it might say something important, something you'd never got round to saying. I *so admired* you. I thought you were Keats and Elijah and the entire damn pantheon of genius rolled into one. I loved you *dispassionately*, if saying it like that is less *embarrassing* for you. Didn't you know that? How could you not know?

They look at each other, eye to eye. SIEGFRIED *breaks the pause. Of the envelope:*

SIEGFRIED. Shall I take it back?

*

Craiglockhart. RIVERS *appears carrying a suitcase. Patients gather and applaud.* ANDERSON *steps forward and clasps* RIVERS*'s hands.*

ANDERSON. We're all very sorry to see you go, you can take my word for it. I was hoping to introduce you to my wife, but unfortunately her train has been delayed.

RIVERS. Very good luck to you, Captain Anderson.

SISTER ROGERS *appears, pushing* WILLARD *in his wheelchair.*

WILLARD. Ah, Dr Rivers! I was afraid that I might miss you before you left.

Behind him, SISTER ROGERS *gestures to* RIVERS*: 'What can I say?' With caution,* WILLARD *climbs out of his wheelchair and takes a few steps.*

A one, and a two, and a three... The spine is cured! And it's *you* who connected the severed ends. I always knew the massage would do the trick. Thank you, thank you. You are a man of many talents. May I wish you the greatest good fortune wherever your life may take you?

RIVERS. You're very kind.

SISTER ROGERS approaches RIVERS.

SISTER ROGERS. Goodbye, Captain Rivers. I hope you will come back to see us.

RIVERS. I'm sure I shall. Meanwhile…

He addresses the whole group.

…I shall miss you all. I shall be thinking of…

He stops. Takes off his glasses and wipes them with his handkerchief.

Goodbye.

Carrying his suitcase, he turns and takes a long walk out.

*

A waiting room in a barracks. July 1918. WILFRED is waiting on a bench. BILLY comes in, still half-dressed from the preliminary inspection. He sees WILFRED. As he continues getting dressed:

BILLY. Hello! It's the Os and Ps again.

WILFRED doesn't know what he's talking about.

WILFRED. What?

BILLY. Alphabetical order. You're O for Owen, aren't you? I'm P for Prior. You were at Craiglockhart.

WILFRED. Oh, yes. I didn't see you after that.

BILLY. Yes, well they turned me down for France.

WILFRED. Me too.

BILLY. So what did you get?

WILFRED. First I was a skivvy in Scarborough, and now I'm about to be an instructor for raw recruits in Berkhamsted.

I'm here for another medical because it seems my heart is skipping a beat and instructors have all got to be A-one.

BILLY. What for?

WILFRED. I've no idea. What's your medical for?

BILLY. I'm signing up for the draft.

WILFRED. I thought you said they turned you down.

BILLY. That was last year. It's different now. They're planning another Big Push, so there's a chance they'll wave me through if I tell enough lies.

WILFRED. Good luck if that's the appropriate phrase.

BILLY. It's highly appropriate. Fancy a roll-up?

WILFRED. Wouldn't mind.

BILLY *rolls him a cigarette.*

Have you seen any of the others from Craiglockhart?

BILLY. I ran into Burns the vomit-merchant. He's out of the war for good.

WILFRED. That's no surprise.

BILLY. Do you remember Anderson?

WILFRED. With the invisible wife?

BILLY. That's the one. He's on duty on reception at the Red Cross Hospital.

WILFRED. That sounds risky.

BILLY. Yes, he might brain one of the nurses with a golf club. It was him who told me about Sassoon.

WILFRED *feels his stomach lurch.*

WILFRED. What about Sassoon?

BILLY. Haven't you heard?

WILFRED. No, tell me. What?

BILLY. He got shot in the head.

WILFRED *stares at him.*

WILFRED. Was he killed?

BILLY. No, he's alive enough and Anderson says it isn't serious, but he's home for the duration. I'm surprised you didn't know.

WILFRED. I hadn't heard.

BILLY (*pleasantly enough*). You were soft on him, weren't you?

WILFRED. I was. (*Grins.*) I was soft as a sponge cake on him. Nobody minded, did they?

BILLY. Not that I noticed.

WILFRED. Not that I care.

BILLY gives him the roll-up and lights it for him.

Thanks.

He smokes. A door opens and a MEDICAL OFFICER *is there.*

MEDICAL OFFICER. Mr Owen? Quick as you can.

He goes back in, leaving the door open.

WILFRED. I've changed my mind. I'm signing up for the draft.

BILLY. I never thought of you as wanting to go to France.

WILFRED. Can't say I do.

BILLY. So is it only your heart that's skipping a beat? Or is it your brain as well?

WILFRED *grins.*

WILFRED. I believe it's both.

He extends a hand and they shake.

Cheers, Billy.

BILLY. Cheers.

BILLY watches as WILFRED goes through the door and closes it behind him. We hear the 'crump' of shell-blast. Then the sounds of battle are drowned by church bells, cheering, car hooters, and the swoosh and popping of fireworks: it's Armistice Night, November 11th, 1918.

The noise dies down.

*

February 1919: the Chelsea Physic Garden. Day. It's very cold. SIEGFRIED *and* RIVERS *are there, both standing, warmly wrapped up, in civvies. Rooks are cawing. There's a bench.*

Pause.

RIVERS. Have you been writing, Siegfried?

SIEGFRIED. Yes, I have.

RIVERS. About the war?

SIEGFRIED. Mostly about the war. I've got a new collection coming out in March. I'll send you a copy.

RIVERS. Thank you. I shall look forward to it.

SIEGFRIED *looks at the bench and then, as though the action had some meaning, takes a seat, cautious at first and then sitting back.* RIVERS, *noticing this, looks away.*

What a magical place this is. I must have walked past it a hundred times, but it never occurred to wonder what was on the other side of the wall.

SIEGFRIED *quotes:*

SIEGFRIED. 'The Chelsea Physic Garden, founded by the Worshipful Society of Apothecaries in 1722.' Highly exclusive. One needs one's own key in order to get in. I used to come here often in the summer.

RIVERS. Is there any particular reason why you've invited me here in the depths of winter?

SIEGFRIED. It's where Owen and I last saw each other. Last August. I'd just been sent back from France, and the hospital used to let me out in the afternoons. We had strawberries and cream at Osbert Sitwell's house over the road, and then we

came in here and we sat on this… this very bench that I'm
sitting on now.

Pause.

It was a perfect late summer afternoon. The magnolias were
out and there was a shimmering and fluttering in the leaves.
He was serenely happy. When evening came, we had dinner at
the Reform Club and then we walked to where he was staying
in Lancaster Gate and said 'goodbye' on the front steps.

Pause.

I've been wondering if you've heard anything of him lately?
Or *from* him, even?

This question seems so extraordinary to RIVERS *that he is
lost for an answer. When he's recovered from his surprise, he
replies with care.*

RIVERS. Not *from* him, no. Why do you ask?

SIEGFRIED. He used to write to me quite regularly when he
was first in France. I began to feel closer to him than I had…
well ever since Craiglockhart days. But I haven't heard
anything since the Armistice. I can't help wondering if
something's happened to him. I've been quite worried.

RIVERS *sits beside him.*

RIVERS (*gently*). Siegfried, the Armistice was three months ago.

SIEGFRIED. What are you saying?

RIVERS. If you want news of a soldier, there are many places
where you can find it. You can apply to the War Office, you
can look in *The Times* archives, you can ask his family.

SIEGFRIED. I didn't think it was right to worry them.

Involuntarily, he winces at the ridiculousness of this reply.

RIVERS. That makes no sense.

SIEGFRIED. I know it doesn't.

RIVERS. Is it… that you want to be told what happened to him
by me?

Pause.

SIEGFRIED. That's it.

RIVERS. He was shot by a German sniper.

SIEGFRIED. Do you mean he was killed?

RIVERS. Yes, he was killed. It was a week before the Armistice. November the 4th. One of my patients, Billy Prior, was killed in the same assault. I feel acutely responsible for him. And for Owen as well, of course. One learns to get used to such things, but it seems exceptionally cruel for a man to lose his life when he's only a few days away from home.

SIEGFRIED. It was one year earlier to the day that he and I had a farewell dinner in Edinburgh. He read me a poem he'd written. It was tremendously good. And then he got angry with me, although we made it up afterwards. I've guessed for months that he must have been killed, but I found it hard to come to terms with. I don't think I'll ever forgive myself.

RIVERS. It's the war. It breeds some dark infection of guilt that spreads from man to man like a disease. We can't escape it, any of us. I've spent the last four years telling one patient after another that whatever he's blaming himself for isn't his fault. This isn't yours.

SIEGFRIED. But there's something you don't know. There was nothing heroic about my getting wounded. It was a balls-up. I'd been mucking about like a fool in no man's land. Mad Jack behaviour. Then I walked back to the line thinking, 'What a fine fellow I am,' and I stood up straight. I wasn't even wearing a helmet.

RIVERS. Perhaps you wanted to be killed?

SIEGFRIED. Perhaps I did. Or I was vain. Or stupid. One of our lookouts saw me in the dark and he thought I was a Jerry so he shot me. Here.

He shows where it was.

RIVERS. But...

SIEGFRIED. Listen. Owen always said that there must be a poet out there. To honour the men who were fighting. He cared incredibly deeply about that. So when he heard that I was back in England, he got himself sent to France. Because of me.

He buries his face in his hands and cries. RIVERS *watches quietly. After some moments:*

I really thought... I really thought that if I could hear it from you, whom I trust, and even love in a way, then the news of his death might bring some kind of...

He laughs through his tears.

...some kind of healing for me. It would be foul and painful, but it wouldn't be wholly bad. There'd be some consolation.

Pause.

RIVERS. He left his poems. You thought one of them was tremendously good. That isn't nothing.

SIEGFRIED *accepts this suggestion calmly, and with no great joy.*

SIEGFRIED. No, it's not.

RIVERS. Although I don't suppose that's all that you wanted to hear from me.

SIEGFRIED. It will do for now.

Pause.

Shall we take a walk around the gardens before we leave?

RIVERS. You go. I'll wait for you here.

SIEGFRIED *stands and walks away and out of sight.*

RIVERS *pulls his coat around him against the cold.*

Looks out after SIEGFRIED, *whom he can see walking away from him.*

Thinks back into himself. Thinks about the war. Then, thinking about BILLY PRIOR, *he whistles the last few bars of 'After the Ball was Over'.*

End of Play.

www.nickhernbooks.co.uk

facebook.com/nickhernbooks

twitter.com/nickhernbooks